The Gospel according to Shakespeare

The Gospel according to

SHAKESPEARE

PIERO BOITANI

Translated by
Vittorio Montemaggi and Rachel Jacoff

University of Notre Dame Press
Notre Dame, Indiana

University of Notre Dame Press

Library of Congress Cataloging-in-Publication Data
Boitani, Piero.
    [Vangelo secondo Shakespeare. English]
    The gospel according to Shakespeare / Piero Boitani ; translated by Vittorio
Montemaggi and Rachel Jacoff.
        pages cm
    Includes bibliographical references and index.
    ISBN 978-0-268-02235-8 (pbk. : alk. paper) — ISBN 0-268-02235-6 (pbk. :
alk. paper)
    1. Shakespeare, William, 1564–1616—Religion. 2. Bible—In literature.
3. Christian drama, English—History and criticism. I. Montemaggi, Vittorio,
translator. II. Jacoff, Rachel, translator. III. Title.
    PR3012.B6513   2013
    822.3'3—dc23
                        2012048958

To

GORDON TESKEY

and the memory of

FRANK KERMODE

Contents

Note on the Texts   *ix*

Preface to the American Edition   *xi*

Introduction   *1*

CHAPTER 1   Amen for the Fall of a Sparrow   *9*

CHAPTER 2   God's Spies   *25*

CHAPTER 3   Music of the Spheres   *41*

CHAPTER 4   Divineness   *57*

CHAPTER 5   Resurrection   *75*

CHAPTER 6   Epiphany   *89*

Conclusion   *125*

Notes   *133*

Selected Bibliography   *139*

Index   *147*

Note on the Texts

Shakespeare's plays are quoted from the Arden editions, as follows: *Hamlet*, ed. H. Jenkins (1982); *King Lear*, ed. K. Muir (1952) and ed. R. A. Foakes (1997); *Pericles*, ed. F. D. Hoeniger (1963); *Cymbeline*, ed. J. M. Nosworthy (1955); *The Winter's Tale*, ed. J. H. P. Pafford (1963); and *The Tempest*, ed. F. Kermode (1954). All these editions have excellent commentaries. Other editions are listed in the selected bibliography. Other plays are quoted from *The Oxford Shakespeare*, 2nd ed., ed. S. Wells, G. Taylor, J. Jowett, and W. Montgomery (Oxford: Clarendon Press, 2005). The Bible is quoted from the King James version or the New Revised Standard Version, unless stated otherwise. References to Greek and Latin texts are to the Loeb edition.

Preface to the American Edition

For several years I had been thinking of writing a small book with a title like the present one and had indeed written various pieces that dealt with these themes. Confronting Shakespeare, and his last plays in particular, is almost impossible, and to couple him with the Gospels and with the whole of Scripture is definitely foolhardy. Yet they are challenges one can hardly resist, because the texts involved are among the masterpieces of world literature, and the prospect of saying something new about them is indeed irresistible to a critic, especially to one who, like myself, has dealt with similar canonical texts—the Bible and its rewritings, the *Odyssey* and its reincarnations, Dante—and who intended to write a book not only for scholars but also for students and the general public.

This aim had two consequences for the shape the book was to take, one in the plot and one in the method. I started with the plot, being convinced that, from the second section of *Hamlet* onwards, Shakespeare is engaged in developing his own Gospel. Thus, I arranged the plays in a roughly chronological sequence that would constitute my general plot: from *Hamlet* to *King Lear*, where Shakespeare's New Testament is only announced and where faith, salvation, and peace are only glimpsed at from far away, and on to *Pericles, Cymbeline, The Winter's Tale,* and *The Tempest,* where the themes of transcendence, immanence, the role of the deity, resurrection, and epiphany are openly, if often obliquely, staged. The Christian Gospels and the Christian Bible represent the signposts, as it were, of this itinerary. Hamlet's new attitude to life and death after his return from England is signaled by his "There is special providence in the fall of a sparrow," a quotation from Matthew. Lear seems to go one step further when he tells Cordelia that they will "pray, and sing, and tell old tales," and "take upon [themselves] the mystery of things as if they were God's spies." The "old tales" are in fact the romances, from *Pericles* to *The Tempest*, which Shakespeare will produce in the next few years. All of them, like *King Lear*, will involve a father and a daughter figure; all, like *King Lear*, will stage amazing recognition scenes. More of this in the introduction.

My second problem was the way in which I would narrate this plot. It was clear to me, from experiences in classrooms all over the world (England, the United States, and other English-speaking countries included), and from the lectures I had been giving to general audiences, even in public venues and on television, that today's public does not know Shakespeare's plays as well as it did two or three generations ago. One needs, in the first place, to tell the stories, which are by themselves capable of producing endless wonder—tell the stories in detail, because the devil, or God, is hidden in the details. Plot, as Aristotle himself saw (he called it *mythos*), is what gets an audience at a performance. Plot is what keeps up the suspense and eventually produces catharsis, final pain, joy, elation, revelation. Arranging the plot is the supreme trick of the artist and, I think, of today's critic. If you tell a story well while teaching Homer, Dante, Tolstoy, or Conrad, you already are half of the way with your audience.

Only half of the way, however. The other half is to make your theme, and your argument, emerge from the plot and from the verbal texture of a play or a novel, letting the author speak as much as possible—which obviously needs no justification with the likes of Shakespeare, who terrifies and enchants simply by having his characters pronounce certain words in a certain order. By pointing out the recurrence of themes, images, allusions, one then weaves into the text what would seem to be a running commentary but is in fact a kind of continuous meditation. For what, after the plot, draws the critic's attention to these particular works is the mystery they conceal at some key points; and the critic, as well as the audience, wants to know more about it—wants, in fact, to think about it and discover its secret. A string of enigmas will produce thoughtfulness, reflection, further reading into the text, and the need to establish comparisons.

At times, the puzzle need only be indicated to stay in the reader's mind (and heart) and eventually trigger enlightenment. At the very beginning of *The Tempest,* for instance, Ariel tells Prospero that, apart from Ferdinand, and on the other side the sailors, all the other "shipwrecked" human beings on the island (the King of Naples, the Duke of Milan, and their courtiers) are "in the deep nook, where once / Thou call'dst me up at midnight to fetch dew / From the still-vex'd Bermoothes." This is a sudden, non-required excess (there is no logical need for this information) as well as an absolutely wonderful leap of the imagination. Why the Bermudas? And why should Prospero have evoked Ariel to fetch dew, of all things, at midnight? One should enjoy or even feel immense surprise and elation at the use of such an image, then store it somewhere in one's memory, slowly begin to realize that the Bermudas and the New World will construct the other face of *The Tempest*'s Mediterranean island, and just as slowly unravel the mystery of Ariel's calling and his final song of freedom ("Where the bee sucks").

In short, this book has little in common with contemporary Shakespeare criticism. I would like it to be rather like a classroom step-by-step *lectura,* somewhere between the medieval or Renaissance commentary and the modern essay, with my introduction and conclusion providing the framework for the stories within by presenting and summing up the general plot. It is, above all, a narration, which, like music (there is so much music in Shakespeare's last plays), picks up and returns to the motifs of living, generating, dying, and being reborn that form the substance of the unique Gospel according to William Shakespeare.

THE AMERICAN EDITION of this book would not have been possible without the efforts of Vittorio Montemaggi and Rachel Jacoff, who have collaborated in translating it. An earlier version of chapter 3, by Anita Weston, then revised by Noeleen Hargan, has also been used. However, the impulse to produce a translation that would make the volume available to an English-speaking audience first came from Frank Kermode and Gordon Teskey, to both of whom it is therefore dedicated. As with the Italian edition, Nadia Fusini has been a constant and inspiring friend, and the *dea e sapientia* to whom I owe the De Sanctis Prize for it.

Piero Boitani
Poggio Mirteto on the Sabine Hills
24 December 2011

Introduction

yet thou dost look

Like Patience gazing on kings' graves, and smiling

Extremity out of act.

Shakespeare's romances bring good news, and they do so in a most immediate sense, as they all have a happy ending. These late plays constitute *his* good news, *his* Gospel. Although Shakespeare has constantly in mind the Christian Gospels, he composes, as the supreme and free playwright that he is, a testament (these are his last works)[1] that is truly *his:* the New Testament of William Shakespeare.

One must take into account the complexity and variety of the themes and forms that inspire Shakespeare (from pastoral drama to the Commedia dell'Arte, from late antique romance to the dumb show and the masque), as well as the unique and ingenious inclusiveness and the mixture displayed in his works: the syncretic juxtaposition of pagan deities and the biblical God, the combination of magic and religion, the intertwining of politics and passion, and the contrast and complementariness of nature and culture, of Nature and Art. But it is striking that the sequence examined in this book—from *Hamlet* to *The Tempest*—opens with a citation from the Gospels and ends with another. For

Hamlet declares to Horatio, echoing Matthew and Luke, that "There is special providence in the fall of a sparrow"; and Prospero, at the end of *The Tempest*, takes leave from his audience (and so from us) with words that rewrite the Lord's Prayer: "And my ending is despair, / Unless I be relieved by prayer, / Which pierces so that it assaults / Mercy itself and frees all faults. / *As you from crimes would pardoned be, / Let your indulgence set me free*" (emphasis mine).

From the second part of *Hamlet* onwards,[2] Shakespeare is meditating on providence, on forgiveness, and on goodness and happiness, and is doing so in Christian terms. I am not interested in trying to determine—as in fact many critics today are legitimately doing—whether Shakespeare was, either in his last years or at any other point in his life, Protestant or Catholic (he certainly was not Puritan, for he derides Puritans on more than one occasion); whether he believed in Purgatory and transubstantiation; or whether he regarded himself as faithful to the Church of Rome or to that of England. There is contradictory evidence in favor of either hypothesis. For instance, Hamlet's "special" providence seems to derive from the ideas of John Calvin; but no trace of this appears in *The Tempest*, which has the action of providence at its heart. Moreover, it is generally held that Shakespeare uses the Geneva Bible, the great English Protestant translation of 1560; but it seems that he sometimes looks to the Douai-Rheims version (1582–1610), that is, the Catholic translation, and sometimes to the Anglican one, namely, the King James Bible, published in its entirety in 1611.

For a Protestant, for an Anglican, Purgatory does not exist, and yet the ghost of Hamlet's father declares to his son that he is "Doomed *for a certain term* to walk the night / and for the day confined to fast in fires / Till the foul crimes done in my days of nature / are burnt and *purged away*" (emphasis mine). However, there is no sign of such possible Purgatory in *The Tempest*, where there is only talk of Hell and (Earthly) Paradise. It is possible to entertain the hypothesis that in the years following the succession to the throne of the Stuart king, James I, Shakespeare was thinking about a rapprochement between London and Rome. The final scene of *Cymbeline*—where the soothsayer announces the fulfillment of the prophecy according to which "our princely eagle, / Th' imperial Caesar, should again unite / His favour with the radiant

Cymbeline," and in which the English king has his own troops and the Roman troops march together under flanking banners—could be an allusion to the *translatio imperii* from Rome to England, but it could also be seen as the veiled hope of a meeting between the papacy and the Crown (that is, the Church) of England.

These are intriguing questions that, however, I leave to historians, and to historians of culture and of ideas in particular. For I find it just as fascinating to note that that speech by Hamlet, and indeed his life, ends with an *amen,* and that the performance of *The Tempest* should end in the same way, with two *amen*s. And to note that from *Hamlet* and *King Lear* onwards Shakespeare's imagination is dominated by tempests, shipwrecks, pirates, and death by water; by flowers and nature in bloom; by relationships between fathers and daughters and between husbands and wives; by recognitions, revelations, epiphanies, and apocalypses. Interpreted retrospectively, the recognition scene between Lear and Cordelia constitutes an archetype for those between Pericles and Marina, between Imogen and Cymbeline, and between Leontes and Perdita; just as the recognition between Pericles and Thaisa returns in that between Imogen and Posthumus, and between Leontes and Hermione. In *The Tempest,* recognitions are replaced by revelations, but even here a crucial relationship remains, that between a father, Prospero, and his daughter, Miranda.

There are, therefore, profound links between these plays. To follow the development of such links is the task I have set myself in this book. It is, of course, the case that biblical allusions constantly appear throughout Shakespeare's work, and that tempest, shipwreck, and recognition are already all present, for instance, in the enchanting comedy that is *Twelfth Night.* But in the sequence I address, such elements find their place within an overall, "providential" understanding of human affairs and are inserted within a larger vision that I can only define as "theological." They form part of an overall discourse addressing the relationship between human beings and God, and in particular the question of divine justice. Hamlet speaks of "a divinity that shapes our ends" and says that "heaven" helped him. Lear prefigures a future, in prison with Cordelia, as a "spy" of God, and the last part of the play is a pressing discussion of divine behavior within human affairs. Pericles contests the gods, rebukes them, accuses them—and then he invokes them, thanks them, is overwhelmed by their grace, and hears the music of the spheres. In *Cymbeline,* Imogen, disguised as a boy, appears as "divineness," there is a revolt against the gods on the part of Posthumus' ancestors, and to them Jupiter himself responds in a theophany. In *The Winter's Tale* we see the resurrection of Hermione. *The Tempest* presents Prospero as God, Miranda as a goddess, and Ferdinand as a god, with Caliban as the devil. Setebos, a Patagonian god, is invoked in the play, in which the pagan goddesses Iris, Ceres, and Juno had appeared earlier.

Rather than abstract or academic discussions on theodicy (Hamlet is the only one who approaches scholastic disputation), we are presented with life experiences: that is, with discussions that Shakespeare brings to life through what his characters suffer and enjoy in their own lives. In particular, the feeling of the presence of divinity is born initially, in Shakespeare's characters, from pain, from suffering that which is obscure and tragic, and from the experience of death. This is the case for Hamlet, but especially for Lear and Gloucester, and again for Pericles and Leontes. The term *patientia* captures well the meaning of such experiences: the term often means "Passion" (as in the Passion of Christ) and at the same time "patience," the ability to endure. The Passion of Job and of Christ are Lear's, who sometimes recommends patience to himself. Pericles is infinitely *patiens,* and Patience appears as a statue in the recognition between Pericles and Marina: able to contemplate "kings' graves, and smiling / Extremity out of act." Edgar recommends patience in one of the most elevated moments of *King Lear:* the patience of being born and of dying. Endurance emerges as the only possible attitude in *Cymbeline.* Even Paulina, in the last scene of *The Winter's Tale,* continually suggests patience to Leontes, patience in waiting for the miraculous. Moreover, Prospero in *The Tempest* does nothing but command patience: to Ariel, to Ferdinand and Miranda, to Gonzalo and Alonso.

Waiting. Shakespeare imposes this on us, delaying and postponing with the most skillful suspense the happy ending of the romances. But another meaning of waiting is found between the "readiness" for death that comes to Hamlet from the Gospels, and the "ripeness" that Edgar proclaims in *King Lear:* between potency and act, between announcement and fulfillment. The "consummation" Hamlet contemplates before leaving for England, which would be provided by suicide's freeing him (and us) from the evil of living, becomes in *Cymbeline* the "consummation" of the peace that Guiderius and Arviragus wish for Fidele, who, they believe, is dead. But another consummation—that is, fulfillment—is what Lear prefigures in going to prison with Cordelia: together to sing like caged birds, to exchange blessings, to ask each other for forgiveness, to pray, to tell each other old tales, to laugh at gilded butterflies, to take upon themselves the mystery of things and be spies of God.

No such consummation is allowed either to Hamlet or to Lear and Cordelia. But Lear's speech prefigures with great precision what will happen in the romances, which are in fact the "old tales" of which he talks. "Consummatum est" can be exclaimed, as by the Gospel of John's dying but victorious Jesus, only by Pericles, Leontes, Cymbeline, Prospero; and by Marina and Thaisa, Perdita and Hermione, Imogen and Posthumus, Miranda and Ferdinand and Gonzalo. There is, in the final scenes of Shakespeare's romances, a plenitude—a grace—that is found only in the Gospels (and particularly in those of John and Luke) within the post-Resurrection scenes.

"Upon such sacrifices, my Cordelia / The Gods themselves throw incense," announces Lear. Such "sacrifices" are the events of suffering and purification that transform the romances into rituals. For this to happen, four other attitudes are needed alongside patience: repentance, forgiveness, and the reaching both towards one's true self and towards others.

These attitudes appear uncertain at the beginning of our sequence. It is unclear whether Hamlet and Laertes truly forgive each other, if not in dying, and it is certain that Hamlet neither repents of anything nor forgives his uncle. Lear does not forgive his two wicked daughters and, in a process already detailed by the apostle Paul, has to go through folly to reach knowledge of himself; but, during the storm, he shows sudden and intense compassion towards the poor, and he confesses and seeks forgiveness before Cordelia: "Pray, do not mock me: / I am a very foolish fond old man." Pericles needs neither repentance nor forgiveness: he is an innocent and meek Job. But both are necessary in *Cymbeline:* for Iachimo as for Posthumus, the former—an Iago-like figure—guilty of provoking the jealousy of the latter, the latter guilty of having wanted to have Imogen killed. Repentance is also required of Leontes, who is jealous to the point of sending his son and his wife to die and of wishing to eliminate his infant daughter. In the final scenes of *The Tempest*, moreover, repentance and forgiveness dominate, where the latter is inspired in Prospero by his servant, the spirit Ariel, and the former in the end is lacking only in Antonio and Sebastian. In *The Tempest*, however, a further, final step is taken when Prospero brings upon himself evil and sin by recognizing Caliban, "this thing of darkness," as his own.

King Lear and *The Tempest* are tied together by a long thread: the father's request for forgiveness before his child. As Lear and Cordelia are going to prison, the old king tells his daughter: "When thou dost ask me blessing, I'll kneel down; / and ask of thee forgiveness." At the end of *The Tempest*, it is Alonso who turns to his son Ferdinand: "But O, how oddly will it sound, that I / must ask my child forgiveness!" This ability to forget oneself and kneel, offering oneself in humility before others—all the more striking if it is manifest in fathers before their children—is one of the most elevated and valuable features of the good news of the romances.

I attempt, in the following chapters, to follow these movements and their ramifications in the individual plays. But even from our present-day perspective it seems apparent that they delineate a path towards love of God and neighbor that, while uncertain and never fully followed (but then who, apart from the saints, can do so fully?), is nonetheless consonant with evangelical proclamations. Shakespeare's romances are not allegories; they are "old tales," perhaps parables. Shakespeare never explicitly says and never suggests with any clarity that, for example, the negated phantom banquet of *The Tempest* is the wedding feast or the Last Supper of the Gospels. He tells stories, in which Lear and Pericles occasionally appear, indirectly or *in aenigmate,* as Job or Christ; in which Marina takes on the semblance of the Way, the Truth, and the Life; in which Hermione comes back to life, like Lazarus, by virtue of the music that strikes her, *if* those present reawaken their faith; in which Ferdinand and Miranda appear like Adam and Eve. Shakespeare leaves it to his audience and his readers to capture the similarities, the affinities, and the differences.

We thus have to pay careful attention to all intertextual allusions, to both sacred and nonsacred texts. For Shakespeare is too consummate an artist to construct mere equivalences or simple "moralities"; he loves obliquity, stratifying shadows, the juxtaposition of myths, times, and places. Bohemia, let us recall, is placed by him on the sea. The enchanted island of *The Tempest* should be found somewhere between Tunis and Naples but is also, clearly, a shadow of Africa and of the New World. It is the Earthly Paradise and a labyrinth, the Golden Age in the middle of the Mediterranean of the Renaissance, and an Ogygia at the confines of the world. The statue of Hermione was carved by Giulio Romano, a pupil of Raphael who designed and frescoed the Palazzo Te in Mantua, but who, as far as we know, was not a sculptor. Perdita is Perfection, Spring, Nature. The tempests that shatter the ships of the protagonists of the romances are those of Homer and Virgil, and those that threaten the caravels precariously finding their way towards America; and they are also the storm that sinks the vessel on which the apostle Paul attempts to reach Rome, or they are even the primordial chaos of Genesis and the *seara*, the whirlwind, out of which God speaks to Job.

One will not find in the romances Matthew's Beatitudes, the wedding at Cana, the miracle of the loaves and fishes, the Crucifixion, or the Ascension. There will emerge, however, in allusive but relevant fashion, the affliction, the meekness, and the purity of heart of Pericles; the weddings of Marina, Perdita, and Miranda; the growth and multiplication of humankind in *The Tempest;* Lear bound to a wheel of fire; Horatio's wish for the dying Hamlet, that "flights of angels sing [him] to [his] rest"; the grace that infuses everything in the final scene of *Cymbeline;* Hermione's resurrection; Prospero, the god who makes himself man.

Shakespeare's overall design, however, becomes clear. Hamlet faintly sees an uncertain and distant light and reflects on the fate of a sparrow, of human beings, and of himself, as if he were on the threshold of the Scriptures. Lear suffers a Passion, shows compassion towards the poor, comes back to life, imagines a beatific future of prayer, forgiveness, and mutual blessing, and then of song and storytelling and smiling: of simplicity, humility, and taking to himself the mystery of things. Lear, who will shortly see the dead Cordelia and who will himself soon die, prefigures a priest at a divine sacrifice, a prophet of God. Pericles becomes such a figure. Finding Marina again discloses to him the harmony of the cosmos, that which is produced by the movement of the heavenly spheres, singing like angels. Pericles, his wife, and his daughter experience beatitude and the consummation on earth of the kingdom of heaven. The same thing happens with the return to life of Hermione's statue and with the encounter between Ferdinand and Miranda. We find, in other words, Gospels founded on immanence, on earthly realization; we find a foreshadowing of heavenly plenitude, the last word of which is the return of God (of Prospero) to history, to earth, after having taken upon himself, if not the mystery of things, then the responsibility for "this thing of darkness," for the evil of the world.

An integral part of such an overall design is the role played by women. The Gospel according to Shakespeare is wonderfully inflected and proclaimed in feminine form. Even in this case we have a precise trajectory. Ophelia, who could perhaps save Hamlet, is rejected by him and dies. Cordelia, who had actually saved Lear, if only for a few hours, also dies. This is followed by an extraordinary progression in which Marina and Thaisa, Imogen, Perdita, Hermione, and finally Miranda appear as true bearers of grace. Marina, the virgin who is not "of any shores" but is mortal, generates him who generated her, and Pericles becomes the son of his daughter; Marina seems to be a shadow of Mary. Thaisa is she whose lips, when touched by Pericles, make him feel on the verge of dissolving and of disappearing forever. Imogen is the *mulier,* the "mollis aer," the air and "sweet" aura that surrounds with its constancy and faithfulness the whole of *Cymbeline.* Hermione, who redeemed life from death, returns love back to Leontes and blesses their daughter. Miranda gives her love to Ferdinand and discovers a new and beautiful world in the men whom she sees at the play's end.

The Good News that Shakespeare's last plays bring to us—I end here these introductory reflections, and point to their fulfillment in the conclusion of this book—is that we can reach happiness on earth, and that this can be true "eternal life." To be reunited with one's loved ones, to rediscover them and recognize them, constitutes happiness: nothing more than this, but equally nothing less. "To recognize those we love is a god," Euripides' Helen had already said. But to be reunited with one's daughter or to one's wife, after having believed her dead, can make us hear the music of the spheres, can make us dissolve and vanish forever in the nothingness that is everything: it is thus a shadow of beatitude.

CHAPTER 1

Amen for the Fall of a Sparrow

There is special providence in the fall of a sparrow.

What happens to Hamlet during the voyage that should bring him from Denmark to England but then leads him home? What—I ask specifically—happens to him on a psychological, mental, and moral level? What happens to his inner self, his way of thinking? Because, more or less, we know what happens materially. His uncle Claudius— brother of Hamlet's father, usurper of his throne and too-soon husband to his widow Gertrude, Hamlet's mother—is not convinced that Hamlet's seeming madness is, as his courtier Polonius claims, caused by his rejected love for Ophelia. Claudius has watched a play, directed by the prince himself, in which the murder of Hamlet's father—which had been denounced to his son by the father's ghost as having been the work of Claudius—is performed with altered names and a Viennese setting. He is perturbed and frightened by this. He therefore thinks, immediately, of sending his nephew to England, so as to rid himself of him. Hamlet then accidentally kills Polonius, who is spying behind a curtain on his conversation with his mother; Claudius understands that, had he been in that hiding place himself, Hamlet would have stabbed him mercilessly.

This murder gives Claudius one more reason to get rid of Hamlet—a political one, he holds, for people will start murmuring against Hamlet for the death of a person who was much loved. Hamlet knows well, and says so to his mother Gertrude at the end of their encounter, that the voyage to England is a trap. This is indeed the case. At the end of his brief audience with Hamlet, as the latter heads towards the ship escorted by guards and accompanied by Rosencrantz and Guildenstern, the king reveals his plan to us. "Like the hectic in my blood he [Hamlet] rages," and England must cure Claudius. England is in debt towards Denmark. It therefore may not "coldly set / Our sovereign process, which imports at full, / By letters congruing to that effect, / The present death of Hamlet."

England will have to kill Hamlet. The prince leaves. But while the king and queen witness the outburst of madness in Ophelia, and her brother Laertes returns, full of vengeful thoughts towards Claudius (whom he considers responsible for protecting his father's murderer, Hamlet), some sailors arrive who bring to Hamlet's faithful friend Horatio a letter from the prince. In it, Hamlet asks Horatio to see that the sailors are received by the king, to whom they will deliver a message. He also entreats his friend to join him as soon as possible (the sailors will lead Horatio to Hamlet), because he has "words to speak in thine ear" that, even though "too light for the bore of the matter," "will make thee dumb." He then explains what has happened:

> Ere we were two days old at sea, a pirate of very warlike appointment gave us chase. Finding ourselves too slow of sail, we put on a compelled valour, and in the grapple I boarded them. On the instant they got clear of our ship, so I alone became their prisoner. They have dealt with me like thieves of mercy; but they knew what they did: I am to do a turn for them. . . . Rosencrantz and Guildenstern hold their course for England; Of them I have much to tell thee. (4.6.14–28)

As will in fact be revealed, this message relates only half the story. Meanwhile, the sailors carry Hamlet's letter to Claudius, who is conversing with the incensed Laertes. The letter simply says that the prince has returned to Denmark—"naked" and "alone"—and asks for an audience for the following day. He will reveal to the king then "th' occasions of my sudden and more strange return."

This does not actually happen. Instead, much later, after Ophelia's funeral and burial, Hamlet tells Horatio the other half of the story. He confirms the "sea-fight" of which he had written in the letter ("and what to this was sequent / Thou knowest already," he adds, though there is no trace in the play of what actually happened after the encounter with the pirates), but claims that on the night before it, having "rashly" left his cabin in his sea-gown, he had looked for Rosencrantz and Guildenstern, stolen their message, broken the seal, and found Claudius' order to the English to cut off his head as soon as he landed. Showing that document to Horatio, Hamlet then says that he forged— and "wrote it fair"—a new order from the king to execute immediately the bearers of the message, sealing it with his father's seal. "So Guildenstern and Rosencrantz go to't," Horatio comments.

This, then, is what has materially happened to Hamlet during his voyage to England: first, his finding proof that his suspicions were correct and his rapid turning against the two so-called friends who had lent themselves to the king's scheme; then, the encounter with the pirates. However, Hamlet reveals neither to Horatio nor to others what has happened in his inner self.

The Hamlet who left for England was prey to feigned madness and profound melancholy. Even before seeing and speaking to what he says was his father's ghost, Hamlet had told his uncle and his mother that, beyond the "trappings and the suits of woe," he had "that within which passeth show."

> Seems, madam? Nay, it is. I know not 'seems'.
> 'Tis not alone my inky cloak, good mother,
> Nor customary suits of solemn black,
> Nor windy suspiration of forc'd breath,
> No, nor the fruitful river in the eye,
> Nor the dejected haviour of the visage,
> Together with all forms, moods, shapes of grief

That can denote me truly. These indeed seem,
For they are actions that a man might play;
But I have that within which passes show,
These but the trappings and the suits of woe.
                              (1.2.76–86)

Hamlet is ever absolute and precise on the intellectual plane: not appearance, but being. However, he is reserved in public about that which he truly has "within." Nonetheless, when alone, he voices his feelings, in the first of his famous soliloquies, beginning with one of those general, introspective, and melancholic reflections that will become typical of his character. He desires "O that this too too solid flesh would melt, / Thaw and resolve itself into a dew." He laments that God should have forbidden man to kill himself: "Or that the Everlasting had not fix'd / His canon 'gainst self-slaughter!" He feels that "all the uses of this world" are, for him, "weary, stale, flat, and unprofitable"; that the world itself is "an unweeded garden / That grows to seed; things rank and gross in nature / Possess it merely" (1.2.129–37).

Later, after the exchange with the ghost has confirmed what his "prophetic soul" had foreboded, Hamlet returns, this time in the presence of Rosencrantz and Guildenstern, to his particular vision of the world, the radical sense of everything's inanity that afflicts his heart. A man of the Renaissance, a university student at Wittenberg, he cannot but perceive the majestic beauty of the universe and recognize "What piece of work is a man!" But against such considerations there rises his lack of mirth and the fact that "it goes so heavily with my disposition":

I have of late, but wherefore I know not, lost all my mirth, forgone all custom of exercises; and indeed it goes so heavily with my disposition that this goodly frame the earth seems to me a sterile promontory, this most excellent canopy the air, look you, this brave o'erhanging firmament, this majestical roof fretted with golden fire, why, it appeareth nothing to me but a foul and pestilent congregation of vapours. What piece of work is a man, how noble in reason, how infinite in faculties, in form and moving how express and admirable, in action how like an angel, in apprehension how like a god: the beauty of the world, the paragon of animals—and yet, to me, what is this quintessence of dust? (2.2.294–308)

Hamlet is certainly prey to melancholy. He defines the times he lives in to be "out of joint"; he considers it a "cursèd spite" to have been born "to set it right"; and he behaves in strange and bizarre ways because "I perchance hereafter shall think meet / to put an antic disposition on."

But it is a two-faced melancholy: on the one hand are uncertainty, indecisiveness, inaction, paralysis; on the other are absoluteness and originality of thought, logical invention, and metaphysical penetration. One could even think—and Hamlet does indeed think—that the latter determine the former. For example, when the actors arrive in Elsinore, he asks the first player to recite "Aeneas' tale to Dido"—that is, the story recounted in Virgil's *Aeneid* and absolutely central to the Western imagination, of the Greeks' capture and destruction of Troy, beginning with "The rugged Pyrrhus, he whose sable arms, / Black as his purpose, did the night resemble." He then makes the actor continue, prompts him, wanting him to reach Hecuba. "But who, O who had seen the mobbled queen," the actor begins. "The mobbled queen?" Hamlet interjects, immediately followed by Polonius: "That's good; 'mobbled queen' is good." But the first player goes on, full of fervor, telling of Priam's death at the hands of Pyrrhus, of Hecuba's screams. Hamlet is satisfied and dismisses the company, inviting the actors to prepare the *Murder of Gonzago,* to which he himself will add a dozen lines, for the following day. Once Polonius, Rosencrantz, and Guildenstern have left, he remains alone. He then pronounces one of his great soliloquies, reproaching himself for his inaction, comparing the actor's passion for a fiction to his own paralysis before reality, and finally deciding to use a fiction—a play—to force King Claudius to confess the murder of his brother:

> O, what a rogue and peasant slave am I!
> Is it not monstrous that this player here,
> But in a fiction, in a dream of passion,
> Could force his soul so to his whole conceit

That from her working all his visage wann'd,
Tears in his eyes, distraction in his aspect,
A broken voice, and his whole function suiting
With forms to his conceit? And all for nothing!
For Hecuba!
What's Hecuba to him, or he to her,
That he should weep for her? What would he do
Had he the motive and the cue for passion
That I have?

(2.2.544–56)

What, then, is Hecuba to the actor reciting her despair? What is a character of "fiction" to a man made of flesh and blood? Why should he cry for her, given that there is no relationship between them? "All for nothing," Hamlet says. There is no reason to lend to fiction any "passion," to "force" the soul towards "conceit." Hamlet is clearly speaking of theatrical action: why identify with characters on stage? His doubt, so far, concerns acting. Nonetheless, Hamlet formulates it, to begin with, in radical, ontological fashion: "What's Hecuba to him?" What is a mythical and literary character to a man of flesh and blood?

That this is the fundamental question here is clarified in the second part of that same line, when Hamlet, in a seemingly casual and rhetorical fashion, driven perhaps by his own discourse—says: "or he to her." What, he to Hecuba? What is a man made of flesh and blood to an imaginary character? This is a paradox and also an ontological abyss. Yes, certainly, this is still a question pertaining to theatre, but not for that any less paradoxical. What is the actor who recites a part to the character whose affairs he recites? If "Hecuba" is an imaginary character, and therefore represents fiction in general, what sense is there in asking if reality means anything to fiction, as the second half of Hamlet's question seems to imply? If Hamlet poses this question, should we conclude that he is subverting the established order of priorities, presuming not that fiction should reflect nature, but that nature should question itself before the mirror? The idea itself of reality thus breaks into a thousand smithereens.

This uncertainty immediately leads to indeterminacy and inaction. Hamlet continually comes up against the tragic impossibility of an empirical and rational recognition of the ghost's identity and of Claudius' guilt, while it is the recognition of his own inactivity that pushes him to organize the play with which he hopes to procure evidence against his uncle. The comparison with the actor's invention leads to the first step, which ends with the impossibility of speech, a total gnoseological silence right in the middle of the longest and most articulate discourse of the protagonist: "Yet I, / A dull and muddy-mettled rascal, peak / Like a John-a-dreams, unpregnant of my cause, / And can say nothing."

Like Pyrrhus in the actor's story, Hamlet remains "neutral to his will and matter." But the problem lies in the fact that, having recognized that this is the case, Hamlet cannot fathom why it should be so. Once again an unfillable void emerges from his knowledge. Now, just as he is about to leave for England, Hamlet reflects on his inaction. He has seen Claudius kneeling in prayer (the king confesses his guilt, but the prince does not hear him) but has decided not to kill him so as not to send him to Paradise. He begins his meditation from nothing less than the Creation of man, who was not made to live like a brute but rather to pursue knowledge, if not also virtue. The human being has been gifted with "such large discourse," with "godlike reason." It is impossible that this should "fust in us unus'd." But it is precisely the excess of reasoning, the "scruple of thinking too precisely on th' event," that blocks Hamlet even on the threshold of self knowledge ("I do not know why"):

> How all occasions do inform against me,
> And spur my dull revenge. What is a man,
> If his chief good and market of his time
> Be but to sleep and feed? A beast, no more.
> Sure he that made us with such large discourse,
> Looking before and after, gave us not
> That capability and godlike reason
> To fust in us unus'd. Now whether it be
> Bestial oblivion, or some craven scruple
> Of thinking too precisely on th' event—
> A thought which, quarter'd, hath but one part wisdom

And ever three parts coward—I do not know
Why yet I live to say this thing's to do,
Sith I have cause, and will, and strength, and means
To do't.

(4.4.32–46)

Hamlet always speaks of general principles. Here, he starts from the Principle, the Beginning itself, in which—it should now be noted—he seems to believe. But he is not able to see the end. In the most famous soliloquy in the history of theatre, before the disturbing, disastrous conversation with Ophelia, he interrogates himself, in at first precise Scholastic fashion (Hamlet has attended university, where teaching would have certainly been by means of the traditional *quaestiones*), whether to be or not to be. He does not formulate his question following the true sense of his thought: whether to continue living or to kill himself. He chooses instead the philosophical terms of a tradition that reaches back to Parmenides and Gorgias, and which his contemporary, Marlowe's Faustus, seems to know equally well (*Doctor Faustus*, A.1.12): to be or not to be, *on kai me on* (to be *and* not to be), *esse aut non esse*.

Here, more or less, is what Hamlet's question would sound like in a classroom in Oxford, at the Sorbonne, in Bologna, or in Wittenberg: "Esse aut non esse. Haec est quaestio: utrum nobilius sit in animo pati adversitates fortunae, aut pugnare contra et terminare eas. Ad primum dicendum quod dormire, mori, est optima consummatio, quia cum somno mortis finem ponimus malibus cordis et generaliter carnis. Sed contra dicendum quod somnus potest habere somnia, quorum natura in somno mortis, qui est sine sensibus corporis, noscimus":

To be, or not to be: that is the question:
Whether 'tis nobler in the mind to suffer
The slings and arrows of outrageous fortune,
Or to take arms against a sea of troubles
And by opposing end them. To die—to sleep,
No more; and by a sleep to say we end
The heart-ache and the thousand natural shocks
That flesh is heir to: 'tis a consummation

Devoutly to be wish'd. To die, to sleep;
To sleep, perchance to dream—ay, there's the rub:
For in that sleep of death what dreams may come,
When we have shuffled off this mortal coil,
Must give us pause.

(3.1.56–68)

This is not a matter of *bene disserere*, of arguing well, which, as Marlowe's Faustus says, *est finis logices*, is the end of logic. It is a matter of life and death. Indeed, there is no *respondeo dicendum* in Hamlet's *quaestio*, which crumbles in its Scholastic articulation precisely at "the rub" presented by the idea of a dream in death. Hamlet knows no answer. "'Tis," he has just concluded, "a consummation / devoutly to be wish'd." "Consummation," that is, end, but also completeness, according to the words of Christ on the cross in the Gospel of John: "consummatum est" (19:30). Just before dying, John's Christ proclaims that his life and his mission have been fulfilled.

Hamlet, on the other hand, wants to die. Before "the thousand natural shocks" to which flesh is heir, he prefers nonbeing. But he compares dying to sleeping, according to an ancient topos, to which he immediately gives a new twist. "To die, to sleep; / To sleep, perchance to dream." True, if one sleeps, one also dreams. But what kind of dreams could come to us "when we have shuffled off this mortal coil"? Dreams are of the body, of the flesh, of that coil enshrouding us in mortality. And these are the very things that human beings lose when they die. "To dream" thus metaphorically refers to the experiences of the soul after death. And it is precisely imagining these that confounds those who would wish to die: "there's the respect / That makes calamity of so long life." Indeed, who "would bear the whips and scorns of time," the injustice of the world, the prevarications, the rejection of love, the pain of living,

But that the dread of something after death,
The undiscover'd country, from whose bourn
No traveler returns, puzzles the will,
And makes us rather bear those ills we have

Than fly to others that we know not of?
Thus conscience does make cowards of us all;
And thus the native hue of resolution
Is sicklied o'er with the pale cast of thought.

$$(3.1.78–85)$$

Thus fear of death means fear of the something that could be there after death, or of the unknown. Hamlet knows and believes in the Beginning, but he seems to know nothing of the end. It is certainly rather curious that he should declare that no traveler returns from that unexplored land, when he lives in a culture which, since the time of Plato, has proclaimed the immortality of the soul and later affirmed a belief in the resurrection of Christ; and when he himself has just seen the ghost of his father return from the purifying flames of Purgatory.[1] But Hamlet's contradictions are part of the inexhaustible human complexity of the character, and do not actually tarnish the natural logic of his reasoning and emotions. For it is precisely that "dread," that fear and trembling, that paralyzes our mind and renders our thought livid before the prospect of death. There is no answer to the question of the end, if not in the acceptance of its total ungraspability or within the context of religious faith.

THIS, THEN, is the Hamlet who leaves for England. When he returns, he is mysteriously changed. Perhaps he has risked death in retrieving Claudius' letter to the English or during the pirates' attack. He certainly—and literally—touches death with his own hands, when he raises Yorick's skull from the pit and learns that the grave being dug by the two clowns is destined for Ophelia. He is still able to *bene disserere,* to argue well, but the experience of death changes him. He is able, now, to "trace" Alexander the Great, with unstoppable logic, from his death until the present day. Hamlet finds himself with his friend Horatio in the churchyard where the two gravediggers are preparing the pit for Ophelia. He exchanges a series of terrible, sardonic lines with one of them, until the clown takes out of the earth the skull of the court jester, Yorick. How many times had Yorick carried Hamlet on his shoulders, how many times had Hamlet kissed him! And now, what a horrendous image is offered to his memory! "My gorge rises at it," Hamlet exclaims, as he pronounces a pained *ubi sunt* on Yorick's "gibes," "gambols," "songs," and "flashes of merriment." Then suddenly the prince turns to Horatio: "Dost thou think Alexander looked o' this fashion i' th' earth?" "E'en so," his friend replies. "And smelt so?" Hamlet starts again, while throwing Yorick's skull to the ground in disgust.

Up to this point, Hamlet has done nothing but echo ancient meditations on death as the great leveler. Lucian, in his *Dialogues of the Dead* (XII–XIV), cites Alexander himself, and Marcus Aurelius (VI.24) comments on the equality between the dust of Alexander and of his servant. Hamlet then launches into an oblique counterpoint to Plutarch, the author of a famous *Life of Alexander*: in life, the Macedonian had a fair complexion and an odor so sweet that his clothes took on a delicious fragrance, as if they were perfumed.[2] In death, Alexander has the same look as Yorick, and emanates the same stench. But now Hamlet throws himself into his own, very personal argument. He tells Horatio, "Why may not imagination trace the noble dust of Alexander till a find it stopping a bung-hole?" When Horatio responds that to think in these terms would be excessively ingenious, Hamlet presents his unimpeachable demonstration, "with modesty enough, and likelihood to lead it": "Alexander died, Alexander was buried, Alexander returneth to dust, the dust is earth, of earth we make loam, and why of that loam whereto he was converted might they not stop a beer-barrel?" (5.1.205–8).

With an inexorable sequence of steps, the reasoning proceeds through the entire "simile" that, through death and dust, transforms Alexander the Great into a beer-barrel stopper. An excess of ingenuity, nuance, and sophistication—as Horatio, together with any reasonable person, would call it—brings Hamlet close to the emptiness of the gravedigger's *ergo*. Nonetheless, from a logical point of view, the prince's extended syllogism is watertight: the imagination can indeed "trace" the path that leads from A (Alexander) to Bb (beer barrel). It is perhaps here, in this "modesty" and "likelihood," in this probability pegged on humility and suspended over improbability, that Hamlet's inner self comes together.

But a few moments later we see him prey to a fury that for the first time is evident. When he understands that it is Ophelia who is destined for the freshly dug grave, he leaps forward, coming up against her brother Laertes. He now knows his own pain and pronounces with pride his own name, echoing the title he had given to his father's ghost. But most of all he now recognizes before everyone, jumping into the pit, his love for Ophelia:

> What is he whose grief
> Bears such an emphasis, whose phrase of sorrow
> Conjures the wand'ring stars and makes them stand
> Like wonder-wounded hearers? This is I,
> Hamlet the Dane. . . .
> . . . .
> I loved Ophelia. Forty thousand brothers
> Could not with all their quantity of love
> Make up my sum.
>
> (5.1.247–51, 264–66)

It could be that the experience of death and the recognition of his love for the dead girl[3] push Hamlet further along a road already embarked upon. Be that as it may, a little later, when Horatio tries to convince him to heed the forebodings of his heart and therefore to renounce or postpone the challenge with Laertes, Hamlet replies, in a strange oracular fashion:

> Not a whit. We defy augury. There is special providence in the fall of a sparrow. If it be now, 'tis not to come; if it be not to come, it will be now; if it be not now, yet it will come. The readiness is all. Since no man, of aught he leaves, knows aught, what is't to leave betimes? Let be.
> (5.2.215–20)

"There's a special providence in the fall of a sparrow."[4] Commentators rightly recall the Gospel of Matthew: "Are not two sparrows sold for a penny? Yet not one of them will fall to the ground unperceived by your Father" (10:29). But perhaps, alongside the Calvinist *special* providence, Shakespeare also has in mind a parallel passage in Luke, where the sparrows are five (12:6), and which is followed by Jesus calling his disciples to be ready, to the "readiness" of which Hamlet speaks: "Be dressed for action and have your lamps lit. . . . You must also be ready, for the Son of Man is coming at an unexpected hour."[5]

To ABANDON ONESELF to Providence, being ready for death, which can come at any moment: this is the evangelical message. But how can Hamlet be the bearer of such humble wisdom and hold, as he does only a moment earlier, that "There's a divinity that shapes our ends, / Rough-hew them how we will" (5.2.10–11)? From where does this Christian theologizing come to Hamlet?

In the first part of the play, as we have noted, Hamlet had not seen any sense in the world: to him it seemed "an unweeded garden, / That grows to seed," "a sterile promontory," "a foul and pestilent congregation of vapours." No trace, there, of a providential power that might take care of poor sparrows or count all the hairs on our heads. At that point, Hamlet asks himself whether to be or not to be, whether it is better to continue living, bearing all the suffering to which man is subjected, or to hasten death, moving towards it deliberately, killing oneself. "To be or not to be," he questioned then. He now proclaims: "Let be"—let it be so, *amen*. And he will repeat this in the supreme moment, that of death: "Let it be" (5.2.343).

To understand the importance of what Hamlet is really saying with his "amen," it is useful to draw another comparison with Marlowe's Faustus, who declares in his opening soliloquy that beyond logic ("to be or not to be"), medicine, and law, perhaps the best thing is the study of Scripture, of theology. Even Faustus comes up against death, and does so by reading Jerome's Vulgate: "The reward of sin is death," and "If we say that we have no sin / We deceive ourselves, and there is no truth in us," he speaks out loud, citing Paul's Letter to the Romans (6:23) and the First Letter of John (1:8). Faustus derives from this a faultless syllogism (which of course does not account for the fact that, from a Christian perspective, Christ redeems us from sin): we certainly sin, and we therefore must die. But he goes beyond this: "Ay, we must die, an everlasting death." What kind of doctrine is this? he then asks himself. If Scripture and theology preach the inevitable damnation of man, what is their use? Faustus thus concludes by bidding farewell to "Divinity" so as to move on to necromancy: "Che sera, sera / What will be, shall be" (A.1.37).

Faustus cites the Italian saying with deterministic fatalism: in the English translation he offers, he states in effect that what will be will have to be. There is no special providence in his words, no "amen." Faustus is already damned in potency. Hamlet's logic ("If it be now, 'tis not to come; if it be not to come, it will be now; if it be not now, yet it will come"), on the other hand, leads to readiness.

Will it be enough to say that Hamlet is no longer prey to melancholy? And yet, only a moment before turning to Horatio with the evangelical phrase about the sparrow, Hamlet has declared an illness more profound than hypochondria: "Thou wouldst not think how ill all's here about my heart." There seems to be in him a pain of living so radical as to be inexpressible. Neither will it be enough to think that having survived Claudius' plot against him is sufficient indication of "providence." In recounting his experiences to Horatio, Hamlet recalls having sealed the letter to the king of England, which sent its bearers, Rosencrantz and Guildenstern, to their death, with his father's seal, which he had in his bag: "even in that was heaven ordinant," he says (5.2.48). The voyage to England and the events related to it, we are made to understand, have in some way been crucial. But nothing is told to us that could clarify the inner development of the protagonist, from the darkness of his initial doubt towards the uncertain light of the ending. "The rest is silence." The fall of the sparrow seems to be its last landing place.

Hamlet does not go beyond this. He does not place himself in the place of the sparrow itself, as the Psalmist does. Psalm 102 in the Geneva Bible says: "For my days are consumed like smoke, and my bones are burnt like an hearth. Mine heart is smitten and withereth like grass, because I forgot to eat my bread.... I watch and am as a sparrow alone upon the house top" (3–4, 7).[6] But it then adds: "But thou, O Lord, doest remain for ever, and thy remembrance from generation to generation. Thou wilt arise and have mercy upon Zion: for the time to have mercy thereon, for the appointed time is come" (12–13). No, Hamlet watches the fate of sparrows, and of human beings, and of himself, as if he were on the threshold of Scripture. That flights of angels might sing him to his rest is the wish and benediction of Horatio, after the death of his friend. There is no effulgence of faith in the closing scenes of *Hamlet:* there is rather the appearance of a distant light. The special providence in the fall of a sparrow remains a mystery only glimpsed at: perhaps comprehended by the protagonist, never revealed to the audience. Unless, of course, we identify the fall of the sparrow with that of Hamlet: with the death of the hero. *Amen.*[7]

CHAPTER 2

God's Spies

And take upon us the mystery of things,

As if we were God's spies.

Lear is Job and the Christ in whom, in the New Testament, the character of Job finds its figural fulfillment. The Book of Job is, among all the books of the Hebrew Bible—what Christians call the Old Testament—that which has most scandalized the Western mind. There is nothing as extreme in Greek tragedy, with the exception, perhaps, of Sophocles' *Philoctetes* and Euripides' *Bacchae*. Nothing questions divine wisdom and justice as does this part of Wisdom literature, in which God, for no apparent reason other than a bet with Satan, allows the Adversary to take away from his faithful servant—the pious and upright Job, who has committed no sin or transgression—everything but his life: material goods, family, health. One does not find, elsewhere in Scripture or anywhere in classical culture, an equally radical exploration of the total gratuitousness of human suffering or of the existence of evil in the world. The four friends who come to console Job try in vain to offer an explanation, but none is sufficient for human reason and feeling. There is no sin, no justice, no providence that can justify this misery.

And neither does God, whose tremendous Voice in the final chapters thunders from the whirlwind against the accusations of his servant, respond to the questioning in a comprehensible manner. For Yahweh answers Job, who calls him to trial, on a different plane, pointing to another mystery. Job was asking: Why me, why are the good stricken and the wicked exalted, why does a human being suffer and die? Why, in other words, does a sparrow fall? The Lord replies: "Who is this that darkens counsel by words without knowledge? Gird up your loins like a man, I will question you, and you shall declare to me. Where were you when I laid the foundation of the earth? Tell me, if you have understanding" (Job 38:2–4). To the tragedy of evil and suffering, here, now, and always, God answers with the mystery of Creation, with the unfathomable enigma at the origin of being and of existence, with the life of the universe—beautiful and horrendous, good and bad, stars and Leviathan. When Yahweh stops thundering, Job retracts and repents "in dust and ashes," recognizing that God can do everything and that nothing for him is unrealizable: "I have uttered what I did not understand, things too wonderful for me. . . . I had heard of you by the hearing of the ear, but now my eye sees you" (Job 42:3–5). After this, the Lord restores twofold all of Job's material goods, renders him happy with children and grandchildren unto the fourth generation, and blesses his new life, until Job dies "old and full of days" (Job 42:10–17).

Lear's tragedy is less radical but, paradoxically, more extreme. Less radical, because Lear is clearly guilty, at the very least, of carelessness and thoughtlessness: of having wanted to divide his kingdom, and especially of not having been able to recognize Goneril's and Regan's flattery, Cordelia's true love, and Kent's loyalty. More extreme, because it is only for a brief moment that Lear is offered restoration: no human or divine blessing saves him from the death of the newly found Cordelia and of Gloucester, or in the end from his own.

Lear is the tragedy of an old king who on his own initiative divests himself of his kingdom, so as to be able to "unburdened crawl toward death." Tricked by his own narcissism, by the mendacious words of the two wicked daughters, Goneril and Regan, and by the silence of the good daughter, Cordelia, Lear divides the kingdom between the first two and banishes the third (and the loyal Kent, who tries to stop him).

In due course, however, Lear is made to reconsider. Goneril and Regan deprive him of his retinue and finally force him to wander as an increasingly crazed beggar, accompanied only by his Fool and by the disguised Kent, on the storm-tormented heath; while it will be Cordelia, given in marriage to the king of France, who will try to save her father. This main story is intertwined, in mirror-like fashion, with another one. The Earl of Gloucester is tricked by his bastard son Edmund, who convinces him that his legitimate son Edgar is plotting against him; Edgar is thus forced to wander through the deserted land disguised, in nakedness, as the beggar Tom. Gloucester tries to help Lear but, as punishment for this effort, is blinded by Lear's daughters. The two old men meet again in Dover, when Cordelia arrives there with the French troops, and while the bastard Edmund loves and lusts after both Goneril and Regan. Cordelia, who in the meantime has found her father again, is defeated by the army led by Edmund. Lear and his daughter are taken prisoner, and Cordelia is killed. Edgar challenges Edmund to a duel after Gloucester's death and kills him. Lear dies.

Perhaps Lear is Job as lived and imagined in the West,[1] the Job who is reduced to a bundle of sores, deprived of everything, and counseled by his wife to commit suicide: "Curse God and die." This Lear is an exclusively tragic Job, to whom is juxtaposed, as counterpoint, the image of the Passion and Crucifixion of Jesus of Nazareth, who in Christian belief is Job's fulfillment. When, in the fourth scene of the second act, Lear tells Regan, who would deprive him of all his knights, to "reason not the need! Our basest beggars / are in the poorest thing superfluous," there is little doubt that from his words emerges the so-called Joban paradigm, the self-identification of the king with his biblical predecessor, victim of God.[2] "You Heavens, give me that patience, patience I need!— / You see me here, you Gods, a poor old man, / As full of grief as age; wretched in both!" (2.4.273–75).

And yet, almost in the same instant, Lear departs from the Job model by flinging curses with a fury that abandons all patience, and jumps from the "gods" to his daughters:

If it be you [gods] that stir these daughters' hearts
Against their father, fool me not so much

To bear it tamely; touch me with noble anger,
. . . .
. . . No, you unnatural hags,
I will have such revenges on you both
That all the world shall—I will do such things,
What they are, yet I know not, but they shall be
The terrors of the earth.

(2.4.276–78, 280–84)

Lear alternates, as he had done shortly before, between the Passion and the *patientia* of Job and Christ, on the one hand, and the most unbridled fury that Yahweh shows against his enemies in the Hebrew Bible, on the other (2.4.106, 159ff., 162ff., 228).

From this moment onwards, Lear's itinerary will be in constant counterpoint to, and a rewriting of, Job. It is not a coincidence that the words just quoted should immediately be followed by the presentation of the two themes that will dominate the third act: tempest and folly, two aspects of the same universal upheaval. "You think I'll weep," Lear tells his daughters; "No, I'll not weep: / I have full cause of weeping," he continues, while the stage directions give us "Storm and tempest," "but this heart / Shall break into a hundred thousand flaws / Or ere I'll weep. O Fool! I shall go mad" (2.4.284–88). *Patientia* and Passion are about to become *hysterica passio*.[3]

And here he is, Lear, in the midst of the hurricane: he vows to be "the pattern of all patience" (3.2.37) and at the same time he encourages the tempest: he invokes it and convokes it. He is a victim, he is Job: "here I stand, your slave, / A poor, infirm, weak, and despis'd old man" (3.2.19–20): slave of the elements. He is also a disturbing and perverse image of Yahweh, He who commands tempests, He who speaks to Job from the whirlwind, from the *seara'*:

Blow, winds, and crack your cheeks! Rage! Blow!
You cataracts and hurricanoes, spout
Till you have drench'd our steeples, drown'd the cocks!
You sulph'rous and thought-executing fires,
Vaunt-couriers of oak-cleaving thunderbolts,

Singe my white head! And thou, all-shaking thunder,
Strike flat the thick rotundity o' th' world!
Crack Nature's moulds, all germens spill at once
That makes ingrateful man!

(3.2.1–9)

But how different is Lear from Job's God! God, thundering from the vortex of his tempest, evokes his own Creation. Lear, on the other hand, from his hurricane wants destruction (perhaps even of Christian civilization, with its steeples and the cocks surmounting them), a second Flood, the flattening out of Earth, the return of being—of Nature—to nothingness. Lear, here, is to the God of the Book of Job as Othello, in his last scene, is to the God of the Book of Exodus.[4]

Shakespeare, however, always approaches the Bible obliquely. When, later (3.4.158ff.), Lear asks the "noble philosopher," the "learnèd Theban," Edgar disguised as poor Tom, "what is the cause of thunder?" he is repeating Yahweh's questions to Job, but he is doing so as a man who seeks understanding, not as the God who is the creator of thunder. Lear enacts a trial for his daughters, as Job calls God to judgment: but we know that the daughters are actually guilty. We can even bring ourselves to consider the exchanges between Lear and the Fool as hallucinated versions of the dialogues between Job and his friends. We are, however, witnessing the gradual, unstoppable fall of Lear's intellect into madness. The "contentious storm" of the elements becomes—and Lear himself seems to be aware of this—an objective correlative of "the tempest in [his] mind":

Thou think'st 'tis much that this contentious *storm*
Invades us to the skin: so 'tis to thee;
But where the greater malady is fix'd,
The lesser is scarce felt. Thou'dst shun a bear;
But if thy flight lay toward the roaring sea,
Thou'dst meet the bear i' the mouth. When the mind's free
The body's delicate: this *tempest* in my mind
Doth from my senses take all feeling else
Save what beats there. . . .

(3.4.6–14, emphasis mine)

This changes the perspective offered by the paradigm of Job, as it subtly shifts from a Jewish Sapiential context to a Christian one. To understand how things truly are, Lear is forced to lose his reason totally, thus following the model outlined by Paul: "Do not deceive yourselves. If you think that you are wise in this age, you should become fools so that you may become wise. For the wisdom of this world is foolishness with God. For it is written, 'He catches the wise in their craftiness'" (1 Cor. 3:18–19). The citation in Paul comes from the Book of Job (5:13), from the first speech with which Eliphaz responds to Job, who curses the day of his birth. In the same tempest scene, Kent invites Lear to enter the hut for shelter and rest; but Lear, like Jesus in Gethsemane, wants only to "pray, and then . . . sleep." Lear then remembers the poor and understands that he has to make himself like them; as he becomes capable of pity and charity, he understands the possibility of the existence of divine justice:

> Poor naked wretches, whereso'er you are,
> That bide the pelting of this pitiless storm,
> How shall your houseless heads and unfed sides,
> Your loop'd and window'd raggedness, defend you
> From seasons such as these? O! I have ta'en
> Too little care of this. Take physic, Pomp;
> Expose thyself to feel what wretches feel,
> That thou mayst shake the superflux to them,
> And show the Heavens more just.
>
> (3.4.28–36)

Shortly afterwards, when Gloucester's banished and disinherited son Edgar appears as the beggar Tom, the poor about whom Lear was thinking are incarnated in him. In him, in Tom, Lear finds the human being as he is without civilization and comfort: the human being in itself, "a poor bare, forked animal." Lear turns to poor Tom with words that reveal how he is now reaching out towards the essence itself of humankind. This is charity, yes, but also ultimate knowledge:

> Why, thou wert better in thy grave than to answer with thy uncover'd
> body this extremity of the skies. Is man no more than this? Consider

him well. Thou ow'st the worm no silk, the beast no hide, the sheep no wool, the cat no perfume. Ha! Here's three on 's are sophisticated; thou are the thing itself; unaccommodated man is no more but such a poor bare, forked animal as thou art. (3.4.103–11)

Shakespeare rewrites the Old Testament with the New, but does so in his own way, juxtaposing Christ on Job and, with extreme tragic presumption, Lear on both. In *King Lear,* however, there also is the parallel path of Gloucester.[5] When the tempest bursts, Shakespeare makes Gloucester's and Lear's parallel journeys to understanding proceed with scenes that have no equals in Western literature. Gloucester does not realize that Tom is actually his son Edgar when he tells him: "Our flesh and blood, my lord, is grown so vile, / That it doth hate what gets it." Nor does he recognize Kent when he tells him: "Ah, that good Kent, / He said it would be thus, poor banish'd man!" He speaks, in Edgar's presence, of his love for him and of his recent plot: "The grief has craz'd my wits" (3.4.149–50, 167–68, 174). Gloucester is blinded by Regan and Cornwall; and, in the moment in which all is "dark and comfortless," he comprehends the truth: "O, my follies! Then Edgar was abused." He then implores the gods for forgiveness and asks for their blessing on his son (3.7.90–91). Now blind, Gloucester acknowledges that he has no path to follow and is therefore not in need of eyes; and he admits that he stumbled when he could see, exclaiming before his yet unrecognized son: "Oh! dear son Edgar, / The food of thy abused father's wrath; / Might I but live to see thee in my touch, / I'd say I had eyes again" (4.1.21–24).

Gloucester reaches an even more profound understanding. When he speaks to his son, he remembers the mad beggar (that is, Edgar) whom he had seen the previous night in the tempest. The beggar had made him think that man is a worm, and this had reminded him of his son. While he observes that *this* beggar must be able to reason a little, "else he could not beg," Gloucester comprehends the vanity of things, as well as the divine cruelty: "As flies to wanton boys, are we to th' Gods; / They kill us for their sport" (4.1.36–37). Immediately afterwards, when the old man observes that the beggar whom he is asking for guidance to Dover is mad, he again discovers, and murmurs, truth: "'Tis the time's plague when madmen lead the blind." Gloucester thus crawls towards the white cliffs, where he thinks of looking for and of finding death.

But the father's radical pessimism is answered, in his son, by a flash of firmness and hope. Gloucester and Edgar walk towards what the old man, tricked by his son, believes to be a high cliff. Like Lear, Gloucester now discovers poverty and charity (and, together with these, divine "ordinance" and "power"); he offers his purse to the person he still believes to be poor Tom:

> Here, take this purse, thou whom the heav'ns plagues
> Have humbled to all strokes: that I am wretched
> Makes thee the happier: Heavens, deal so still!
> Let the superfluous and lust-dieted man,
> That slaves your ordinance, that will not see
> Because he does not feel, feel your power quickly;
> So distribution should undo excess,
> And each man have enough.
>
> (4.1.64–70)

When they reach what Gloucester believes to be the cliff's edge, Edgar's voice, Gloucester notes, "is altered." Edgar crafts with words the supreme illusion, an imaginary cliff off which his father could throw himself. The old Earl gives up the world and life, shaking "patiently my great affliction off." He hurls himself and falls . . . to the ground. Gloucester truly experiences a sort of death and resurrection (according to a pattern which we will find again in the romances); for after his fall that is not a fall, he encounters another Edgar, who affirms Gloucester's life to be a miracle, calls him "father" for the first time, defines Tom as a "fiend," and, referring to how the gods "make them honours / Of men's impossibilities"—in short, by constructing another reality out of words and illusion—gives him the gifts of memory, of a new self-consciousness, of a new life. "I do remember now," Gloucester says, finally accepting *patience:* "henceforth I'll bear / Affliction till it do cry out itself / 'Enough, enough,' and die" (4.6.75–77).

THE TWO STORIES approach and touch each other. When mad Lear appears on the scene again, Gloucester has completed his catharsis, while the king still has not. The first recognition scene happens now, between Gloucester, who in his blindness has regained a kind of reason, and Lear, who is still looking for it. Recognition is, here, precisely the encounter and the fusion between two different kinds of consciousness: or, as Edgar says in talking to Lear, "O, matter and impertinency mix'd; / Reason in madness!" While Gloucester recognizes Lear almost immediately as soon as he hears his voice, the king continues to seek his truth. He says that "Gloucester's bastard son / was kinder to his father than my daughters / Got 'tween the lawful sheets." An instant later, when Gloucester wants to kiss his hand, Lear, in another moment of illumination, replies: "Let me wipe it first; it smells of mortality." The exchange between the two is characterized by this continuous alternating movement between personal point of view, contact with the other, and leaping towards universal truth. Gloucester comments on Lear's words by saying: "O ruin'd piece of nature! This great world / Shall so wear out to naught." He immediately adds: "Dost thou know me?" And Lear recognizes him: "I remember thine eyes well enough."

This is recognition in an oracular and oblique form. Lear does not say, "yes, I recognize you," but he affirms that he remembers well Gloucester's eyes. His memory captures precisely the core of the Earl's new awareness, his new, suffering existence: his eyes. And it is on these eyes that Lear fixes his attention until such insistence produces its own truth and forces Gloucester to enter into the language of apparent folly: "yet you see how this world goes," to which the Earl responds: "I see it feelingly."

This is true knowledge, without a doubt, and true wisdom, which does not need sense perception or syllogistic reasoning. This wisdom is based only on experience and on the ability to construct a parable, to capture truth in ordinary life: "Thou hast seen a farmer's dog bark at a beggar?" Lear constantly ruminates on his primary question, that of regal authority: the concept of justice is turned upside down and the old king, who finds mercy in himself, absolves all his persecutors: "None does offend, none, I say none. I'll able 'em." He then continues to strike where it hurts: on the eyes. It is at this point that, finally, after a delay which has become unbearable, there is complete recognition: "If thou wilt weep my fortunes, take my eyes. / I know thee well enough: thy name is Gloucester." Such recognition transforms Lear into a preaching prophet and brings to light a profounder truth, already rooted in human nature; it leads—in a renewed invitation to patience—to re-cognition:

> Thou must be patient; we came crying hither.
> Thou know'st the first time that we smell the air
> We wawl and cry. I will preach to thee: mark.
> . . . .
> When we are born, we cry that we are come
> To this great stage of fools.
>
> (4.6.180–85)

LEAR IS LATER given nothing less than a resurrection: that which, astonished, we witness when we see him come to his senses and recognize Cordelia in the French camp near Dover (4.7). Before approaching this scene, however, let us bear in mind how Shakespeare has already allowed, three scenes earlier, for Cordelia to be identified, in an indirect but precise way, at the moment in which she spurs those at her service to look for her father. "O dear father," she exclaims, "It is thy business that I go about" (4.4.23–24). The phrase is an extraordinary cast of the words in the Geneva Bible that Jesus addresses to Joseph and Mary, who, after looking desperately for him, finally find him among the teachers in the temple: "How is it that ye sought me? Knew yee not that I must goe about my Father's business?" (Luke 2:49). Then, one of the gentlemen who tries to bring Lear a message from Cordelia, speaks of her in these terms: "Thou hast one daughter / Who redeems nature from the general curse / Which twain have brought to her" (4.6.206–8). Cordelia is thus Daughter in the same way in which, in the Gospels, Jesus of Nazareth is Son.

The process through which Shakespeare brings Lear back to life, purified and accepting his newfound existence, is a miracle of dramatic art. The king's descent into madness and the acquisition of wisdom had been slow and alternating. The actual resurrection is, by comparison, much quicker, but Shakespeare is not in a hurry to reach the father's recognition of his daughter; rather, he crafts a delay that is all the more extraordinary in being concentrated into only a few lines. First, Cordelia speaks to Lear with the eagerness of a subject: "How does my royal lord? How fares your majesty?" Lear's voice emerges from the depths of the abyss, suspended between his hell and his daughter's paradise. As the Fool's prophecy concerning the wheel is fulfilled, Lear sees in Cordelia a blessed soul, a breath of Heaven. Such recognition transcends the world only immediately to be plunged again into consumed flesh: "You do me wrong to take me out o' th' grave; / Thou art a soul in bliss; but I am bound / Upon a wheel of fire, that mine own tears / Do scald like molten lead" (4.7.45–48). This is a *Pietà*—made of unbounded emotion.

When Cordelia asks him, "Sir, do you know me?" Lear replies, again, "You are a spirit, I know. Where did you die?" Then, Lear becomes aware of space and time: but these are still clouded, sunk in confusion, in uncertainty. It is in fact his sense perception itself that is still suspended: he is not able to swear that these are his own hands; he feels the puncture of a pin on his skin but would like to be certain about such a sensation. Cordelia implores him for his blessing. Lear kneels. Then in twelve hesitant and tortuous lines, he completes the recognition, feelingly, as it were. He begins from the only certain data, his age and his madness; but he is worried that he is not perfectly in his senses. He thinks that he recognizes his daughter and Kent, but still he doubts this. He understands that he has lost memory of himself and the world because he has lost cognition of space, of his clothes, and of time. Then, in an instant of sudden illumination, he finally recognizes Cordelia, precisely at that moment in which he realizes he is (still, only, and fully) a man:

> Pray do not mock me:
> I am a very foolish fond old man,
> Fourscore and upward, not an hour more or less;
> And, to deal plainly,
> I fear I am not in my perfect mind.
> Methinks I should know you and know this man;
> Yet I am doubtful: for I am mainly ignorant
> What place this is, and all the skill I have
> Remembers not these garments; nor I know not
> Where I did lodge last night. Do not laugh at me;

For, as I am a man, I think this lady
To be my child Cordelia.
                              (4.7.59–70)

All is suspended in the wonder of this beatific scene: memory and
being, knowing and living, madness and wisdom. "Forget and forgive,"
Lear will shortly implore. Recognition thus means, in the instant between past, present, and future, a new awareness, an opening of the
mind towards the other, which contrasts with Lear's previous falling in
on himself. That earlier kind of knowledge was the all-too-human wisdom of madness: this present knowledge, which is forged by the earlier
one through a wheel of fire, is communion; it is a fully human wisdom,
sublimed and purified by acceptance.

If, as we have seen, Cordelia is Daughter as, in the Gospels, Jesus of
Nazareth is Son, then it is her father who comes back to life; and in the
moment in which he comes out, as he puts it, of his tomb, he identifies
himself with the Christ of the Passion: "Thou art a soul in bliss; but I
am bound / Upon a wheel of fire." In this father and this daughter, divinity is both divided and fused; in this moment, Cordelia is Jesus as-
cended into Heaven ("bliss" suggesting the happiness of Paradise), Lear
is Jesus on the cross. When the father finally recognizes his daughter in
recognizing himself as man—"For, as I am a man, I think this lady / To
be my child Cordelia"—she fully proclaims herself as Daughter; and, as
Jesus does, she declares at the same time her own, absolute being: "And
so I am, I am" (4.7.46).[6]

A unique rewriting of Scripture, indeed, in which an old man, who
could have appeared as God the Father, is resurrected in front of the
Son! But it does not end here; it ends in the third scene of the fifth act,
when, after the defeat of the French army, Lear and Cordelia are taken
to prison. The daughter invites the father to go and "see these daughters
and these sisters," Goneril and Regan. It is perhaps an attempt at
reconciliation, an invitation to forgiveness. Lear refuses without hesitation; his mind shuts itself in the prison, in a cage into which the outside
world only penetrates through the mind and sensations of the prisoners, through the exclusive perception of the self. Knowledge, locked in
contemplation, becomes recognition of the world within oneself and

divine knowledge; as if the self in communion with only one other "you" is elevated to become a "spy" of God:

> No, no, no, no! Come, let's away to prison;
> We two alone will sing like birds i' th' cage:
> When thou dost ask me blessing, I'll kneel down,
> And ask of thee forgiveness: so we'll live,
> And pray, and sing, and tell old tales, and laugh
> At gilded butterflies, and hear poor rogues
> Talk of court news; and we'll talk to them too,
> Who loses and who wins; who's in, who's out;
> And take upon us the mystery of things,
> As if we were God's spies: and we'll wear out,
> In a wall'd prison, packs and sects of great ones
> That ebb and flow by th' moon.
>
> (5.3.8–19)

Lear imagines a future of redemption and transcendence, which, while fully human, reaches well beyond the resurrection foreshadowed earlier. It is a future with a monastic appearance, a sacral aura: how deeply moving to imagine the daughter imploring a fatherly blessing, and the father invoking the daughter's forgiveness! It is also a future of prayer, of song, of storytelling, of smiling; of simplicity, humility, and detached but beatific knowledge of both natural and political reality, from the smallest, splendid detail of *being* ("gilded butterflies") to the swinging motions of *becoming* (the "court"). But above all, in this familial paradise, Lear and Cordelia will together fulfill their mission as *human beings* separated from, but in harmony with, God: "And take upon us the mystery of things, / As if we were God's spies."

Lear and Cordelia resemble Jesus: like him—like all human beings, from a Christian perspective—they too are sons of God. Beyond this, however, they are his "spies." Theirs will not be an exploration of the world but an assumption of the mystery of the world. To accept the responsibility for all that is: this is burden of the prophet, of a "spy" of God; of anyone who, on God's behalf, wishes to scrutinize the spirit and the affairs of human beings, and of anyone who, like the prophet

Habakkuk (2:1), places himself or herself as a sentry watching out for what God will say, how God will reply to his or her laments. "Upon such sacrifices, my Cordelia, / The Gods themselves throw incense" (5.3.20–21). Sacrifice: in the sense of someone offering a sacrifice while at the same being sacrificed, immolated and made sacred; but made such—that is, blessed, sanctified—by God himself, like Christ.[7]

Lear sees himself and Cordelia, the imprisonment to which they are subjected, and the death to which they will certainly be condemned, as holocausts: according to the Pauline formulation, living and holy sacrifices, pleasing to God (Rom. 12:1). Theirs is therefore a path of Passion, which ends—potentially—in transfiguration.

It is here that the Gospel according to Shakespeare takes its first form: an eminently poetic Gospel, as Lear and Cordelia will sing and will tell each other old tales. It is a Gospel that is as close to the canonic ones as Lear and Cordelia resemble the Christ who takes upon himself the evil of the world; and that is as far from the canonic Gospels as Lear and Cordelia are different from Christ in taking upon themselves the *mystery* of things.

We know, of course, that this, which Hamlet would call "a consummation / devoutly to be wished," is not allowed to Lear and Cordelia: that in fact in this tragedy, resurrection is followed by death; and that nothing is further from the end of the Book of Job and from the Gospels than the end of *King Lear*. Shakespeare's rewriting of Scripture is, however, complex as always. The story that has Gloucester as protagonist ends in a subtly different way. Gloucester thinks and, as we have seen, says that "As flies to wanton boys, are we to th' Gods. / They kill us for their sport." This is responded to, after the fiction of the suicidal jump off the cliff, by the beggar, who is turning into Edgar again: "therefore, thou happy father, / Think that the clearest Gods, who make them honours / Of men's impossibilities, have preserved thee" (4.6.72–74). Edgar, like Hamlet in his final scenes, glimpses a higher design. In Gloucester's fake fall, as in the sparrow's real one, there is a special providence: "Thy life's a miracle," Edgar tells his father. To Hamlet—for whom *the readiness is all*—Edgar replies, later, with a thought specular to his, and more complete: *the ripeness is all* (5.2.11). Readiness is not enough: one needs ripeness. All should be "consummatum," fulfilled.

Human beings, Edgar says, have to "endure" exit from this world as well as entry into it: they have to be ready to die but also ready to be born, and to be born again; in short, to accept life. *Endure:* like Job learns to do; as Christ does.

This message, which Edgar brings with him to the end of the play, declaring that "The weight of this sad time we must obey," could seem insignificant in the face of the many, unbearable catastrophes of *King Lear*'s closing scenes; but it is no different from the message of Ecclesiastes, who recognizes the vanity of things and yet holds that there is a time for tears and one for joy and laughter. It is from here, from the scene of recognition and resurrection between Lear and Cordelia, that Shakespeare will embark upon the "old tales," upon the songs of the romances, where Cymbeline and Imogen, Pericles and Marina and Thaisa, Leontes and Perdita and Hermione, Prospero and Miranda— fathers and daughters, husbands and wives—lose themselves, fall, endure, find themselves again, and are resurrected. The fall of a sparrow will thus be replaced by the flight of angels. The transfiguration denied to Lear will thus take place. And such will be—earthly and fully immanent, and yet a shadow of the metaphysical, of the divine—the New Testament of William Shakespeare.

CHAPTER 3

Music of the Spheres

This, this: no more, you gods!

Pericles opens under the dark shadow of incest, and with an escape. The Prince of Tyre's misfortunes begin when he goes to Antioch to try to win the hand of King Antiochus' daughter by solving a riddle. If he does not succeed, he will be condemned to death. However, realizing the dreadful secret of the incest between father and daughter, Pericles finds himself being chased by a murderer sent by Antiochus and returns to Tyre, where he entrusts Helicanus with the task of ruling Tyre and then flees (like Jonah) to Tarsus, which is ruled by Cleon and Dionyza and is currently devastated by a terrible famine. Pericles helps Tarsus with food from his ship. After receiving a letter from Helicanus calling him back to his country, he sets sail for Tyre. A fierce storm leaves him shipwrecked. Reduced to rags, he is washed up on the shore of Pentapolis, where the waves also throw up the armor left to him by his father on his deathbed. With this armor he takes part in a jousting tournament to win the hand of Thaisa, daughter of King Simonides of Pentapolis. Thaisa falls in love with him, and the two marry. Another message arrives from Helicanus, calling Pericles back to Tyre once more. The pregnant Thaisa insists on boarding the ship alongside her husband, but it is hit by a storm, during which Thaisa gives birth to a daughter and then dies.

Pericles is above all a tale of infinite mishaps at sea. T. S. Eliot commented that when he read it, he had "a sense of a pervading smell of seaweed" from start to finish.[1] Shakespeare, of course, did not invent the story but borrowed it from a medieval poet and, in the final analysis, from a late antiquity romance and from the legend of a saint, Mary Magdalene. Between Pericles and Mary Magdalene there is a tenuous but fascinating connection. *Pericles* is the dramatic version of the story, passed on through a hundred different renditions and languages, of Apollonius of Tyre. (Shakespeare simply changes the names, but he refers explicitly to the tale about Apollonius written by the fourteenth-century poet John Gower in the *Confessio Amantis,* with Gower himself also appearing in the Chorus of the play.)

But in the Middle Ages there was a splendid contamination between the adventures of Apollonius and those of Magdalene. In Jacobus de Voragine's *Legenda aurea,* for example, Magdalene, now sister to Martha and Lazarus and a sinner par excellence, washes Jesus' feet with her tears, dries them with her hair and anoints them with precious oil, repents, witnesses the Crucifixion, anoints the body of Jesus after his death, and is the first to see the Lord resurrected. Thirteen years after the Ascension, Magdalene, Lazarus, Martha, and others are made to board a ship by the unfaithful and are cast into the waves. Divine will, however, enables them to reach Marseilles, where Magdalene preaches faith in Christ. Before converting, the head of the province and his wife want Magdalene to perform a miracle to make the lady fertile. When the wife finds herself pregnant, her husband decides to visit Peter in Rome to verify that the Christian truth corresponds exactly to what Magdalene preaches.

Going against all attempts to dissuade her, the woman insists on accompanying her husband. Blessed by the saint, man and wife set off on their journey. On the second day, however, there is a dreadful storm, and the woman dies in childbirth on board the ship. The sailors want to throw her body into the sea to placate the waves, but the husband sees to it that his wife and child, covered by a cloak, are left on a "hill" that arises from the sea. Cursing Magdalene for what has happened, he continues on to Rome, where Peter advises him to bear patiently his wife's "sleep" and that of the child resting alongside her. He reassures the husband that just as the Lord gives, takes, and returns, so He will be able to transform his tears into joy.

Two years later, instructed in the faith by Peter and having visited Jerusalem with him, the man sets sail for Marseilles. He stops at the hill where he had abandoned his wife and son and finds a child playing on the shore. The frightened boy runs to take shelter under the cloak covering his mother's body and sucks milk from her breast. The man then recognizes his wife and child and invokes Magdalene to make her breathe again. The miracle takes place, and the three of them return to Marseilles, where they recount everything to Magdalene before she withdraws into a hermitage in Aix-en-Provence. In England, the story was also staged in the late Middle Ages as a sacred play with the title *Mary Magdalen*.

The core of the story of Apollonius and of Shakespeare's Pericles presents clear parallels with this secondary plot of the legend of Magdalene. Pericles' wife, Thaisa, insists upon accompanying him to Tyre, and she dies giving birth to Marina on board the ship during a storm. Thrown into the sea (like Jonah, because of the sailors' superstitions) in a coffin containing enough items to identify her, Thaisa is restored to life (the first time this motif appears in the play) through the music and medicine of Cerimon in Ephesus, where she withdraws to Diana's temple. Pericles leaves the infant Marina in Tarsus with Cleon and Dionyza. Years later, consumed by envy, Dionyza decides to have Marina murdered, but before this can happen, some pirates (recalling Hamlet's pirates) kidnap her and sell her to a brothel at Mytilene. But the young girl refuses to do what she is told and manages to move to a household where she earns her living by singing, doing needlework, and teaching the daughters of noblemen. Meanwhile, Pericles returns to Tarsus for his daughter, but Cleon and Dionyza show him the grave where they claim she has been buried. Desperate with grief, Pericles dresses in sackcloth, lets his beard and hair grow unkempt, and travels across the sea in a daze, until he reaches Mytilene, where a mysterious young girl who sings beautifully is brought to him in an attempt to cure him.

Naturally, Shakespeare's version (Shakespeare's in spite of the well-known "collapse" of the text) inserts this plot within a framework that is even more romance-based than that of the legend of Magdalene, namely, the framework of Apollonius. Guided by the ancient voice of Gower that links the various episodes within his tale, and enlightened by the pantomimes that silently clarify several of the plot's intricate intersections, spectators and readers follow Pericles on his sea voyages as he is tossed by the waves and by Fortune, gripped by divinities that are incomprehensible but whose actions in the end turn out to be providential. Pericles is a Job who suffers everything: a "man of sorrows, and acquainted with grief," one of the afflicted, the meek, and the merciful spoken of in the Beatitudes (Matt. 5:3–12).[2] All sorts of trials befall him, as happens to the characters of late-antiquity romances and to medieval knights: the riddle and escape, saving Tarsus from famine, endless sea voyages, shipwreck, the tournament, the loss of his wife in another storm, the presumed death of his daughter. Throughout all these trials he acts with vigor, nobility, generosity; he puts up with everything right up to the last, the visit to Marina's grave. Then, as with Lear after the abuse he suffers, Pericles too "bears / A tempest, which his mortal vessel tears, / and yet he rides it out"—lost within himself, his conscience forgotten in grief, allowing "his courses to be ordered / By Lady Fortune" (4.4.29–31, 47–48).

The first part of the adventures of Pericles is in effect dominated, materially and ideally, by Fortune: he himself thanks her for helping him to find his lost armor, and the Chorus (Gower) attributes the storm that takes place while Thaisa is giving birth to the vagaries of Fortune (2.1.37, 122; 3.1.46). The various ups and downs reduce Pericles to a Nobody: a poor man worn out by the stars and the elements like Lear; a human being who has forgotten what he was. He is simply, as he tells the fishermen at Pentapolis, overcome with need, hunger, and cold, and he wishes only to die in peace:

> Yet cease your ire, you angry stars of heaven!
> Wind, rain, and thunder, remember, earthly man
> Is but a substance that must yield to you;
> And I, as fits my nature, do obey you.
> Alas, the seas hath cast me on the rocks,

Wash'd me from shore to shore, and left me breath
Nothing to think on but ensuing death.
Let it suffice the greatness of your powers
To have bereft a prince of all his fortunes;
And having thrown him from your wat'ry grave,
Here to have death in peace is all he'll crave.

. . . .

A man whom both the waters and the wind,
In that vast tennis-court, have made the ball
For them to play upon, entreats you pity him;
He asks of you, that never us'd to beg.

. . . .

What I have been I have forgot to know;
But what I am, want teaches me to think on:
A man throng'd up with cold. My veins are chill,
And have no more of life than may suffice
To give my tongue that heat to ask your help;
Which if you shall refuse, when I am dead,
For that I am a man, pray see me buried.

(2.1.1–11, 59–62, 71–77)

Unlike Lear, however, Pericles obeys the forces of destiny.[3] In doing so, his virtues come to the fore: he is "good in conversation," "benign," modest to the point of considering himself to be "like a glow-worm in the night, / The which hath fire in darkness, none in light" (2 Chorus, 3, 9; 2.3.43–44). He speaks like the Scriptures and feeds the hungry (2 Chorus, 12; 1.4.85–96).[4] Pericles is the "meek" of the Gospels, of the Sermon on the Mount.

In the second part of his adventures and misfortunes, Pericles shows that he is also pious: he invokes and interrogates the gods. For example, when the ship that is taking him to Tyre with Thaisa in labor is tossed by the storm, he turns to the gods of the sea and the wind, and then to Lucina, protectress of childbirth:

The god of this great vast, rebuke these surges,
Which wash both heaven and hell; and thou that hast
Upon the winds command, bind them in brass,

Having call'd them from the deep! O, still
Thy deaf'ning, dreadful thunders; gently quench
Thy nimble, sulphurous flashes!
. . . .
. . . Lucina, O
Divinest patroness, and midwife gentle
To those that cry by night, convey thy deity
Aboard our dancing boat; make swift the pangs
Of my queen's travails!
                                    (3.1.1–6, 10–14)

Neither the elements nor the gods reply, however, and "the seaman's whistle / Is as a whisper in the ears of death, / Unheard." When the reply arrives, it announces, through the midwife's lips, the death of Thaisa and the birth of the tiny infant Marina whom she holds in her arms. Pericles' "piètas" and resistance suffer their first blow. While Lychorida repeatedly urges him to show "patience," he questions the very honor of the gods, inferior to that of men, who do not take away what they have given:

O you gods!
Why do you make us love your goodly gifts,
And snatch them straight away? We here below
Recall not what we give, and therein may
Use honour with you.
                                    (3.1.22–26)

Nonetheless, turning to the newborn baby and wishing her a life that is easier than her birth, Pericles entrusts her to the "best eyes" of the "good gods"; and later, at Tarsus, when he speaks with Cleon and Dionyza about his dead wife, he recognizes that "we cannot but obey the powers above us": if he too "could . . . rage and roar as doth the sea she lies in, yet the end must be as 'tis." Like the romance hero, like Jesus of the Gospels, Pericles accepts *telos*, the preestablished end and purpose. Only when he is given the news that "all his life's delight," Marina, flesh of his flesh, the daughter that should now be in full bloom, is dead, Pericles, like Job, dresses in sackcloth and lets himself go.

Pericles, who had already become a Nobody after the first ship-wreck, dies an inner death. His wife and daughter are dead to him. And in reality Thaisa does pass through death, and Marina approaches death when she is almost murdered and later ends up in a brothel. But as we have seen, Thaisa is resurrected, thanks to Cerimon's music and medi-cine, and decides to devote her life to Diana. And Marina grows up. Time passes, marked out by Gower in his role as the Chorus and de-scribed by Pericles as "the king of men," "their parent," and "their grave" (2.3.44–45). And now, the first time we see Marina is when she wants to scatter flowers on the grave of Lychorida, her nurse:

> No, I will rob Tellus of her weed,
> To strew thy green with flowers; the yellows, blues,
> The purple violets, and marigolds,
> Shall as a carpet hang upon thy grave,
> While summer-days doth last. Ay me! poor maid,
> Born in a tempest, when my mother died,
> This world to me is as a lasting storm,
> Whirring me from my friends.
>
> (4.1.13–20)

Flowers, which will also make their appearance in *The Winter's Tale* and *Cymbeline,* are the tangible, colorful, and marvelous signs of perishing and persisting, suspended between memory and the present, between the tempest and the grave. The pious Marina commemorates the dead and enhances their death with life, while she remembers that her own life is nothing but a storm: like that of Pericles, like that of every human being, according to the traditional topos.

Marina survives the pimps' plans for her, thanks to her language, which, as Lysimachus says, expresses her virtue and goodness (4.6.108, 112).[5] She manages to keep clients at bay simply by speaking, by entic-ing them to purity. As Gower tells us at the start of the last act, Marina "sings like one immortal, and she dances / as goddess-like to her ad-mired lays"; with her wisdom "Deep clerks she dumbs," and "with her needle composes / Nature's own shape, of bud, bird, branch, or berry, / That even her art sisters the natural roses" (5 Chorus, 3–7). Marina is the divinity of art and learning, a creating and enchanting Spring, *Life.*

LITTLE BY LITTLE, during the last act, she also becomes the Way and the Truth. The recognition scene between Marina and her father, described by T. S. Eliot as the greatest recognition scene ever written and a perfect example of the "ultra-dramatic," "a dramatic action of beings who are more than human,"[6] takes place in an atmosphere that recalls the fourth Gospel. Marina is introduced to Helicanus as a creature who could, with her sweet harmony, enchant Pericles and open up a channel in his dulled senses, like a miracle worker and at the same time supreme *kalokagathia* (let us note the words themselves, which add a veil of Platonism over the evangelical echoes), "all goodness that consists in beauty." Convinced by Lysimachus, Helicanus allows Marina to board the ship where Pericles lies in a dazed state, wrapped in sackcloth, his hair and beard long and unkempt. Everything is set out in such a way that a new *Pietà*, following that of Cordelia and Lear, takes shape. Marina goes up to him, singing and encouraging him to listen to her, but he replies with an unconscious mumble ("Hum, ha!") and ignores her. Then Marina speaks, saying that she is a young maiden who has never before invited eyes, even though admired like a comet, someone who has put up with suffering equal to his, yet of noble birth, now reduced to a slave of the world and one of its "awkward casualties." Receiving no reply, she thinks of desisting, but something (an unknown, mysterious "something") illuminates her face and whispers to her to remain until he speaks.

And Pericles speaks, spluttering something that repeats her words and asking her to explain what she means. Marina has given him back speech. Now, she awakens his confused memory and his still sluggish conscience. Pericles asks her to turn her eyes to him (as though she were a divinity) because she is, he says, "like something that—." Suddenly, a fleeting memory makes him ask: "What countrywoman? / Here of these shores?" Marina's answer is perfectly natural, truthful, and at the same time mysterious and allusive to a superior being: "No, nor of any shores; / Yet was I mortally brought forth, and am / No other than I appear" (5.1.103–5).

Marina is precise: she is not from Mytilene or any other shore because she was born at sea. But "nor of any shores" suggests an ultra-terrestrial origin, and Marina quickly adds that she was brought into the world "mortally" and ends by humbly pointing out that she is nothing other than what she appears to be. A *being* that coincides perfectly with *appearing?* A being that comes from no shore, from no land, yet was born of a mortal woman? Only the Jesus of the Gospels can claim such fullness and such an origin.

Barely awakened from his long period of oblivion, "great with woe," Pericles remains on earth. He notes the resemblance between the young girl and his wife—the broad forehead, the same height (*to an inch*), the same "wand-like" straight stature, her silver voice, her "jewel-like" eyes, her pace like Juno, her enchanting speech that makes people wish for more. His questions quicken: Where do you live? Where did you grow up? How did you learn these extraordinary arts? "Where I am but a stranger," replies Marina to his first question. And then, in answer to the others: "If I should tell my history, 'twould seem / Like lies, disdain'd in the reporting." Still both human and superhuman. Pericles is now ready to *believe*. The woman before him is Pallas, Wisdom, Justice, *Truth:*

> Prithee, speak;
> Falseness cannot come from thee, for thou look'st
> Modest as Justice, and thou seem'st a palace
> For the crown'd Truth to dwell in. I will believe thee,
> And make my senses credit thy relation
> To points that seem impossible; for thou look'st
> Like one I lov'd indeed.
>
> (5.1.119–25)

Superhuman, yes, but rooted in the most human sentiment there is, love, and love for a wife. Believing, yes, but believing with the senses: finding the resemblance through physical appearance. Pericles has to make the same effort as did Magdalene before the resurrected Christ, whom she mistook for a gardener. To him, Thaisa and Marina are dead, and to recognize them he must pass through the mystery of death and overcome it. Without giving up on reason, facts, evidence, signs—your relatives, your ancestry, your birth family, your suffering, your history— Pericles continues:

> Tell thy story;
> If thine consider'd prove the thousandth part
> Of my endurance, thou art a man, and I
> Have suffer'd like a girl; yet thou dost look
> Like Patience gazing on kings' graves, and smiling
> Extremity out of act. What were thy friends?
> How lost thou them? Thy name, my most kind virgin?
> Recount, I do beseech thee. Come, sit by me.
>
> (5.1.134–41)

We have two parallel Passions, that make the man and woman, father and daughter, like a shadow of the Christian God, a single person. But it is the daughter who now embodies the infinite capacity of suffering and forbearance: *patiens* like Jesus on the Cross, and at the same time a statue of Patience—like those of the funeral monuments of the time—placed at the graves of kings, at the grave of *this* king, Pericles. This is an image that is both active and passive at the same time: forbearance, and a smile that annuls extreme misfortune; Olympian contemplation, and com-passion; a detached and restorative smile. *Patience*—so often invoked, recommended, and hinted at—is now a statue, alive, of flesh and blood: Marina.

The young girl replies only with a name, like Jesus calling Magdalene "Mary" in John's Gospel: "My name is Marina." Pericles exclaims (echoing Lear when he recognizes Cordelia): "O, I am mock'd, / And thou by some incensed god sent hither / To make the world to laugh at me" (5.1.142–44). Pericles starts to perceive the divine in recognition. But Marina, and Shakespeare, invite patience. Every statement by the girl is an oracle, a riddle that gives rise to further questions. The game of recognition is slow, gradual, and protracted, in order to highlight the joy, the pleasure of recognition as theorized by Aristotle and Freud.[7] Patience, yes, like that which smiles on the graves of kings. Slowly, Marina continues: "The name / Was given me by one that had some power, / My father, and a king." When Pericles is taken aback, and now puts together the shreds of signs that this revelation brings, the young girl stalls: "You said you would believe me; / But, not to be a troubler of your peace, / I will end here." So the question is, once again, to believe or not to believe:

> But are you flesh and blood?
> Have you a working pulse, and are no fairy
> Motion? Well, speak on. Where were you born,
> And wherefore call'd Marina?
>
> (5.1.152–55)

To believe, however, one must recognize, reestablish the continuity of being-in-reality, identify the *being-this-here,* go through death: finding neither ghost nor fairy, but pulse, flesh, blood, movement—a live person. Everything must click: "Call'd Marina / For I was born at sea." Marina does not clarify whether or not she is of flesh; she simply evokes her birth at sea, far from all shores. But for Pericles the sea is now becoming *that* sea: who was your mother? And when Marina replies that her mother was the daughter of a king and died just as she gave birth, Pericles, repeating what he has just said a few moments earlier, shows his final hesitation: "This is the rarest dream that e'er dull'd sleep / Did mock sad fools withal; this cannot be / My daughter, buried" (5.1.161–63). It is easier to believe a dream, of course: one does not survive death. Yet this dream speaks, moves, tells marvelous yet coherent tales. Pericles asks for more details, promising to listen in silence till the end, and to *believe* every syllable she utters. Marina procrastinates again; then, while he weeps, she tells her story, ending with her father's name: "I am the daughter to King Pericles, / If good King Pericles be."

And now the gradual revelation, the delayed epiphanies, become knowledge, but not immediately, not directly. Pericles calls Helicanus and asks him if he knows who is this girl who has made him weep. Unaware of Marina's identity, Helicanus calls on Lysimachus, the governor of Mytilene. But when he too states that he does not know, it is Pericles himself who has to fulfill, simultaneously, the recognition and an act of faith. Pericles feels invaded and almost overcome by the sea that had so tormented him. This sea is now happiness. As Euripides' Helen says, *to recognize those we love is a god*:[8]

> O Helicanus, strike me, honour'd sir!
> Give me a gash, put me to present pain,
> Lest this great sea of joys rushing upon me
> O'erbear the shores of my mortality,

And drown me with their sweetness. O, come hither,
Thou that beget'st him that did thee beget;
Thou that wast born at sea, buried at Tharsus,
And found at sea again. O Helicanus,
Down on thy knees! thank the holy gods as loud
As thunder threatens us: this is Marina.

(5.1.190–99)

Marina has risen: born at sea, buried on land, and brought back to life again by the sea. Pericles has risen and becomes, almost in Dantean fashion, his daughter's son (5.1.205–7),[9] the extreme opposite of Antiochus' incestuous relationship with which the play began. Marina is presented as the shadow of Christ who has become man, his mother's father: "godlike perfect" and "another life" for her father, as Pericles says a couple of lines later. Marina is the *Way* and the *Life*, therefore, yet also of flesh and blood, daughter of Thaisa, as she herself replies to the final question in her father's intense interrogation, thus providing the definitive proof.

Pericles, and Shakespeare, are careful to leave the theological implications in subtle balance and full ambiguity: Helicanus must kneel and thank the holy *gods*. And now it is Pericles who, after revealing his name to her, is risen, becomes father once more, blesses her, asks for new clothes, and consecrates Marina as his daughter, as though she were the Spirit that in the form of a dove pronounces upon Jesus: "This is my beloved son, in whom I am well pleased" (Matt. 3:17):

Now, blessing on thee! rise; thou art my child.
Give me fresh garments. Mine own, Helicanus,
She is not dead at Tharsus, as she should have been,
By savage Cleon.

(5.1.212–15)

Father and daughter are becoming, as Lear wished for himself and Cordelia, God's spies: because they have taken upon themselves, they have experienced and experience, the "mystery of things." Pericles then fully regains his consciousness, becomes aware of the world around him, and in the end recognizes himself: *I am wild in my beholding.* He is transfigured, in the throes of ecstasy.

As soon as this last step in knowledge has been taken, the shadow of the ultra-terrestrial returns. Pericles asks again for his robes, invokes the heavens' blessing on Marina, and suddenly hears music: "But hark, what music?" he asks. He then resumes talking, asking Marina to relate everything, "point by point," to Helicanus, who seems still to doubt. Then he stops again: "But, what music?" When Helicanus replies that he hears no music, Pericles exclaims "None? The music of the spheres! List, my Marina." Seeing the others incredulous, he repeats: "Rarest sounds!" Then the heavenly music prods him, enchants him, makes him feel drowsy:

> Most heavenly music!
> It nips me unto listening, and thick slumber
> Hangs upon mine eyes: let me rest.
> (5.1.231–33)

A thousand years earlier, Pericles had played for King Simonides, Thaisa's father, a "sweet music," a "delightful pleasing harmony" (2.5.26, 28). Along with his cloths and fire, Cerimon at Ephesus had used music (as will Paulina in *The Winter's Tale*) to bring Thaisa back to life (3.2.86–89). At the beginning of this scene, Marina plays and sings. Now, only Pericles perceives this transcendental music, which "renders a metaphysical 'listening' physical."[10] Heavenly music is not just any kind of harmony; according to an ancient doctrine, it is produced by the celestial spheres as they are moved by the angels. Human beings no longer hear it, either because they are inured to it from birth, or because it is abstract, purely rational, or because they are prevented by the flesh. Dante hears it clearly in Paradise. But it is mentioned only one other time in Shakespeare's works, in *The Merchant of Venice*, when the Christian Lorenzo, after ordering music to be played, invites the Jewish Jessica to contemplate the stars:

> How sweet the moonlight sleeps upon this bank!
> Here will we sit and let the sounds of music
> Creep in our ears: soft stillness and the night

Become the touches of sweet harmony.
Sit, Jessica. Look how the floor of heaven
Is thick inlaid with patines of bright gold:
There's not the smallest orb which thou behold'st
But in his motion like an angel sings,
Still quiring to the young-eyed cherubins;
Such harmony is in immortal souls;
But whilst this muddy vesture of decay
Doth grossly close it in, we cannot hear it.

(5.1.58–65)

Neither Lorenzo nor Jessica hears this music because they are still locked within the body's "muddy vesture of decay." But because they possess immortal souls, they know that it is there, and that such harmony befits "soft stillness," the night and their love. Pericles, on the other hand, is able to perceive it. He is in a state of grace, beyond the merely human, although still completely a man. As Dante put it, "trasumanar significar per verba non si poria" (*Par.* 1.70–71): passing beyond humanity cannot be put forth in words. It can only be suggested by means of images, like this one of celestial music.

Thus, Shakespeare proposes knowledge of the flesh and, in the flesh, experience of the ultra-terrestrial, that which is beyond life. To recognize those we love is now truly a god. Shakespeare rewrites Greek romances and the stories of Euripides with his mind illuminated by John's Gospel. Philologically, this is absurd, but it holds a truth and has the sense of literature. Shakespeare seems to be divinely inspired. The idea is the only critically coherent one in its human and theological enormity, but it should be formulated as follows: Like John, Shakespeare does everything to make us believe that he is divinely inspired.

AGAIN REWRITING Greek romance and Euripides with an eye on the Gospels, Shakespeare, to bring the play to an end, makes Diana, *ex machina*, appear in a vision to the sleeping Pericles, in which she tells him to go to Ephesus, make sacrifices at her altar, and reveal to the priestesses there all his and his daughter's "crosses." In the following scene, the pious Pericles promptly does so, thus causing his wife Thaisa to faint upon hearing his tale.

Here too, however, Shakespeare employs delaying tactics. While Thaisa immediately recognizes Pericles' voice and appearance, he needs an intermediary and proof of hers. Cerimon, who had restored Thaisa to life after her body had arrived at Ephesus, now reveals to him that this priestess of Diana is in reality his wife, as Pericles' own account in the temple indicates; then Cerimon mentions the "jewels" found in her coffin, and this provides the final proof. In his Gospel, John is rather reluctant to have the apostle Thomas touch Jesus. Shakespeare, while making use of material evidence, has no intention of using this alone. As she faints, Thaisa exclaims: "Voice and favour! / You are, you are—O royal Pericles!" When she recovers, it is again Pericles' voice and appearance that strike her, and it is her voice invoking his name—like that of Jesus with Magdalene—that pierces his heart: "O, my lord, / Are you not Pericles? Like him you spake, / Like him you are. Did you not name a tempest, / A birth and death?"; and Pericles: "The voice of dead Thaisa!" (5.2.13–14, 31–34).

Thaisa is resurrected from the dead a second time. Pericles does not hear, this time, the music of the spheres, nor does he fall into a slumber, but he does experience the extreme threshold between living and dying, between "the fullest realization of happiness and the disappearance of all."[11]

> This, this: no more. You gods, your present kindness
> Makes my past miseries sports. You shall do well,
> That on the touching of her lips I may
> Melt and no more be seen. O come, be buried
> A second time within these arms.
>
> (5.3.40–44)

This is the supreme moment: reuniting with his wife, putting his family back together again, and perpetuating it (Lysimachus and Marina will marry, announces Pericles) coincide with recognizing divine action, in which kissing a woman's lips means dissolving, and burying her in his arms means "no more [to] be seen," where the most human gesture of love and union that subverts death is one with going beyond and transfiguring it. The time is *this,* now, on the earth. The thing is *this one* here, at the theatre. This is the Gospel preached by William Shakespeare.

CHAPTER 4

Divineness

Behold divineness

No elder than a boy.

In *Cymbeline,* Shakespeare performs a series of extraordinary theatrical experiments, combining and juxtaposing genres: history, love story, the tragedy of jealousy, and pastoral elegy. Here too, however, the action is dominated by death and ends in rebirth, in recognition, and in the re-constitution of *philia*—of affections and of love. On its primary level the play attempts to unify the flow of both Roman and universal history (while *Cymbeline* describes a pagan world, it is set at the time of Christ's birth and life) and to coordinate them with the Celtic beginnings of British history.

Encouraged (if not prompted) by the queen and by her son Cloten, Cymbeline, king of Britain, refuses to pay the tribute to Rome, an ac-tion that represents a first, forceful affirmation of British national iden-tity. For this to be confirmed, a victory must be won against the Roman punitive expedition. Playing a role of fundamental importance in this war, beyond the duty imposed on them by bonds of lineage and loyalty, are Cymbeline's sons Guiderius and Arviragus, their putative father Belarius, and the king's son-in-law Posthumus Leonatus. All of these characters contribute in the hour of need to laying the foundation for a new, independent Britain.

The peace that follows, however, has surprising consequences. Cymbeline decides of his own accord to once again pay the tribute to Rome and to accept the rule of Augustus Caesar; and, more significantly, he has the British and Roman troops march together in triumph, their banners waving "friendly together" in the wind, towards the temple of Jupiter, where the newly established union will be ratified.

In a harmony "tuned" by the "the fingers of the powers above," the grand prophetic vision announced by the soothsayer before the battle is thus fulfilled, and is expanded upon in the last scene of the play: "For the Roman Eagle, / From south to west on wing soaring aloft, / Lessen'd herself and in the beams o' the sun / So vanish'd; which foreshadow'd our princely eagle, / Th' imperial Casear, should again unite / His favour with the radiant Cymbeline, / Which shines here in the west" (5.5.471–77).[1]

This is an unexpected perspective, in the context of the increasingly deep separation between Elizabethan England and the contemporary empire of Catholic Rome. (Scholars have, indeed, proposed that Shakespeare is here adapting to new attitudes emerging with the rise to the throne of James I.) It is also, rather appropriately, a very enigmatic vision, if one interprets it as saying that the Roman eagle flies westward towards an apotheosis which is also a sunset, and that it is precisely there in the West that the sun, which is "radiant Cymbeline," now shines, as if the former is handing authority over to the latter, thus prefiguring an ideal continuity with Britain's new *imperium* in the West. The history of the two worlds of the past, the classical Roman one and the Celtic-English one, is thus prophetically taken into a vision of the present and the future.

Upon this historical drama is grafted the drama of the play's heroine, which entails an unfolding of all the principal kinds of human relation and affection: father-daughter, wife-husband, rejected lover-beloved, sister-brothers. The pure Imogen, daughter of Cymbeline, has preferred marriage with Posthumus Leonatus, a man of noble descent but poor, to marriage with Cloten, son of the king's second wife. Cymbeline banishes Posthumus and thunders in rage against Imogen, with the same vehemence with which Lear lashes out against Cordelia. While in exile in Rome, Posthumus praises Imogen's beauty and her faithfulness, which is, however, called into question by Iachimo. The two thus make a bet: if Iachimo wins Imogen's honor, Posthumus will give to him the ring he wears on his finger. Iachimo travels to Britain, courts Imogen, is rejected, and returns to Rome, where he presents his adversary with a series of apparently convincing proofs of his wife's betrayal. Posthumus decides to have Imogen killed by his servant Pisanio, who, however, spares her. Dressed as a boy, she is then found by General Caius Lucius, leader of the Roman troops against Britain. After the Roman defeat, Imogen finds herself at Cymbeline's court, where she proves to Posthumus that he has been tricked by Iachimo.[2]

Juxtaposed to this forceful story of jealousy (in the first part of which Iachimo is astute and malicious like Iago, and Posthumus is impulsive and violent like Othello) is a further story that underscores a senseless male brutality. Cloten, an obtuse bully whom the queen would like to see marry Imogen so as to acquire power through royal succession, is firmly rejected by the king's daughter. When she flees from the court to escape both him and her father and to rejoin her husband, Cloten, dressed in Posthumus' garments, pursues her and vengefully threatens to rape her and to kick her back to her father. In an attempt to discredit Posthumus before Imogen, Iachimo had accused him of seeking sexual gratification in "lips as common as the stairs / That mount the capitol," with a "satiate yet unsatisfied desire" that, "ravening first the lamb, / Longs after for the garbage." These are, in fact, Iachimo's own cravings, making his whole conversation with Imogen (the lamb) an inordinately violent act of rape.

Even Imogen's relationship with her brothers is subject to eros. When she disguises herself as a boy with the significant name of Fidele (both "faithful" and "loyal": "Thy name well fits thy faith, thy faith thy name," says the Roman general Lucius) and finds refuge in the mountains, near the dwelling of Belarius, Guiderius, and Arviragus, Guiderius declares that, were he a woman, he would immediately start courting her, while Arviragus decides to love her as a brother.

Imogen is thus caught within a complex web of male desires that on the conscious plane manifest themselves as a continuous "rating" of her honor and virtue and that fill the play with monetary and economic images. But Imogen, the object of everyone, is *Cymbeline*'s supreme subject: she is the highest point of reference for the play's other actors and for its audience. Her love for Posthumus is constant and passionate. Her filial devotion is irreducible. Her behavior with Guiderius, Arviragus, and Lucius is gentle. Her resistance before the queen, Cloten, and Iachimo is proud and luminous. Imogen's presence, her human, feminine, and moral depth, imparts to the story its defining characteristics: *Cymbeline* does not simply present us with historical and erotic drama, but also with pastoral drama and elegy, with the tragedy and comedy of knowledge, and with the mystery of a romance about transcendence.

Even on a first approach, be it at the theatre or on the page, the most fascinating scenes of *Cymbeline* are those taking place in the mountains (presumably of Wales) in front of or around the cave where Belarius, Guiderius, and Arviragus live (3.3, 6, 7; 4.2, 4). The background to the fable-like plot is presented as follows: Belarius, a noble and valiant member of Cymbeline's court, has been banished by the king; with the help of the nurse Euriphile, who will later become his wife, he kidnaps Cymbeline's two infant sons and raises them in the mountains, calling them Polydore and Cadwal, concealing from them their true identity, and praising the simple life they lead as closer to nature and to communion with heaven than court life could ever be. But the princes' youth and blood (their "nature," as Belarius puts it in astonishment) betrays their true origin. "Out of your proof you speak," Guiderius declares, "we poor unfledg'd, / Have never wing'd from view o' th' nest; nor know not / What air's from home. Haply this life is best / . . . to you / . . . but unto us it is / A cell of ignorance, travelling a-bed, / A prison, or a debtor that not dares / To stride a limit." And Arviragus, in the same scene, insists: "What should we speak of / When we are as old as you? When we shall hear / The rain and wind beat dark December? . . . / We have seen nothing: / We are beastly: subtle as the fox for prey, / Like warlike as the wolf for what we eat: / Our valour is to chase what flies: our cage / We make a quire, as doth the prison'd bird, / And sing our bondage freely" (3.3.27–44).

Within this debate between youth and old age, court and country-side, civilization and nature, experience and ignorance, innate impulses and reason, the appearance of Imogen-Fidele acts as a catalyst, introducing into the scene grace, gentleness, and the highest femininity. As the mountain dwellers Arviragus and Guiderius immediately realize, Fidele sings like an angel and cooks divinely: "Nobly he yokes / A smiling with a sigh; as if the sigh / Was that it was, for not being such a smile; / The smile mocking the sigh, that it would fly / From so divine a temple, to commix / With winds that sailors rail at. / . . . grief and patience, rooted in them both, / Mingle their spurs together" (4.2.51–58). Fidele is thus noble, saintly, angelic, divine, and once again a supreme human example of patience.

When, after having drunk the potion that Pisanio has been given by the queen, Imogen-Fidele apparently dies (like Juliet had done with tragic consequences, and like many other heroes and heroines of ancient romance), a pastoral drama is transformed into doleful elegy. The old man and the youths are perturbed by the sudden appearance of the divine breath that illumines their male and quasi-animal hunting life. When Imogen presents herself before them as Fidele, they mistake her for a "faery," then an angel, and finally a deity: "Behold divineness / No elder than a boy," Belarius exclaims when he sees her for the first time.

Divineness: the word refers not to the person of a deity but to the divine "nature," the essence of a god. This is *Cymbeline*'s central affirmation. It matters not in what guise it veils itself (we can recall Athena in the guise of a shepherd in the *Odyssey*, when Ulysses wakes up in Ithaca and fails to recognize her). The essence of the divine transpires in any case; it reveals itself mysteriously (as an epiphany, like an infant in a manger), and it irradiates an aura of incomprehensible grace, as if it were the smile of things.

Then, when Imogen dies, both the old man and the youths enter the lyrical dimension so typical of Shakespeare's late plays. Imogen-Fidele has lent them feminine grace: so much so that the two young mountain dwellers are brought to pronounce the floral elegy that in *Pericles* and *The Winter's Tale* is the prerogative of two maidens, Marina and Perdita. Belarius now comprehends melancholy: "O melancholy, /

Who ever yet could sound thy bottom, find / The ooze, to show what coast thy sluggish care / Might'st easil'est harbour in? / Thou blessed thing, / Jove knows what man thou mightst have made; but I, / Thou diedst a most rare boy, of melancholy" (4.2.203–8). And Arviragus thus describes the sleep of death in which he found Fidele: "Stark, as you see: / Thus smiling, as some fly had tickled slumber, / Not as death's dart, being laugh'd at" (the smile, precisely) (4.2.209–11). Even the harder Guiderius, who has just killed Cloten and thrown his head into the stream, calls the boy "sweetest, fairest lily" and invokes the fairies, that they may hover over Fidele's tomb. And Arviragus, in response, picks up on the floral imagery, developing it with the intense subtleness and refinement of the romances:

> With fairest flowers
> Whilst summer lasts, and I live here, Fidele,
> I'll sweeten thy sad grave: thou shalt not lack
> The flower that's like thy face, pale primrose, nor
> The azur'd harebell, like thy veins: no, nor
> The leaf of eglantine, whom not to slander,
> Out-sweeten'd not thy breath: the ruddock would
> With charitable bill, (O bill, sore shaming
> Those rich-left heirs that let their fathers lie
> Without a monument!) bring thee all this;
> Yea, and furr'd moss besides. When flowers are none,
> To winter-ground thy corse.
> (4.2.218–29)

Finally, accompanying Fidele's corpse to the tomb, Arviragus and Guiderius together recite a dirge, as if they were the women in traditional scenes of lamentation over the dead Christ. It is a moving and soulful *memento mori,* and simultaneously a hopeful wish for serene "consummation" and fulfillment.

GUIDERIUS
Fear no more the heat o' th' sun,
  Nor the furious winter's rages,

Thou thy worldly task has done,
  Home art gone and ta'en thy wages.
Golden lads and girls all must,
As chimney-sweepers, come to dust.

ARVIRAGUS
Fear no more the frown o' th' great,
  Thou art past the tyrant's stroke,
Care no more to clothe and eat,
  To thee the reed is as the oak:
The sceptre, learning, physic, must
All follow this and come to dust.

GUIDERIUS
Fear no more the lightning flash.
ARVIRAGUS
  Nor th' all-dreaded thunder-stone.
GUIDERIUS
Fear not slander, censure rash.
ARVIRAGUS
  Thou hast finish'd joy and moan.
BOTH
All lovers young, all lovers must
Consign to thee and come to dust.

GUIDERIUS
No exorciser harm thee!
ARVIRAGUS
Nor no witchcraft charm thee!
GUIDERIUS
Ghost unlaid forbear thee!
ARVIRAGUS
Nothing ill come near thee!
BOTH
Quiet consummation have,
And renowned be thy grave!
                    (4.2.258–81)

This is the lesson of death: painful, but serene. Death erases all trouble and worry—the wrath of the powerful, the oppression of the tyrant, slander, censure. It recalls Hamlet, the Hamlet of "to be or not to be," who wanted suicide. Death, for everyone, is to return to dust. It is the end of joy but also of pain. And death is also "home" and "wages," fulfillment of earthly cares, of all our worldly tasks. That deity—Imogen-Fidele—was not immortal. She was extremely human, yet she smiles in death, like the statue in *Pericles* of Patience on the tomb of kings. A farewell is now given to her that is both valediction and benediction: may she not be touched by ills and unburied ghosts. *Cymbeline* responds to *Hamlet*. The Prince of Denmark wished to sleep forever, to die: this was, for him, "a consummation / Devoutly to be wished." Now Guiderius and Arviragus wish the dead Fidele a "quiet," serene, tranquil "consummation." They then strew flowers on the grave, uttering words that echo Job: "The ground that gave them first has them again: / Their pleasures here are past, so is their pain."

THIS ELEGIAC VISION, however, is not allowed to take over, let alone conclude, *Cymbeline*. Good theatre demands otherwise. As soon as Guiderius and Arviragus finish their song, Imogen wakes up, next to Cloten's body (still clothed in Posthumus' garments). This is a climactic moment in the contrast between appearance and reality and in the struggle for knowledge that pervades the play. Imogen's senses revive, she sees the bloody corpse, and her consciousness realigns itself with memory, going back to the moment preceding her sleep ("I thought I was a cave-keeper, / and cook to honest creatures," she exclaims, perplexed). Nonetheless, the impression that gains strength in her is that of mere appearance, of a dream: "But 'tis not so: / 'Twas but a bolt of nothing, shot at nothing, / Which the brain makes of fumes. Our very eyes / Are sometimes like our judgements, blind" (4.2.299–302). The contact with reality betrays consciousness, but in turn that reality entails illusion, generates misunderstanding: the dead Cloten is mistaken by Imogen for Posthumus, an error that in *Romeo and Juliet* would lead to tragedy.

Cymbeline is brought to this threshold of tragedy by that other knot of misunderstanding, which dominates the first part of the story, in which Iachimo convinces Posthumus that he has in fact won Imogen's honor. The principal scene in this respect (2.4) constitutes a classic case of logical discourse based on a distorted presentation of "circumstances." The discussion begins with Iachimo affirming that he has brought back with him to Rome "knowledge" of Imogen. The meaning of the term ("knowledge" in the carnal sense) imparts to the whole dialogue an emotional charge that immediately transports it beyond any mere forensic, rational, or neutral analysis. At stake is the knowledge on which the bet depends, and with it therefore (from a male perspective) the very honor of Posthumus himself and the life of Imogen. As Posthumus specifies, "If you can make't apparent / That *you have tasted her in bed,* my hand / And ring is yours" (emphasis mine). Iachimo thus spins the web of persuasion with the ability of a consummate sophist: first he will present the "circumstances," which, "being so near the truth" (note the depth of ambiguity in his words), will lead his interlocutor to "believe"; the validity of such proofs will then be confirmed by the oath he will swear as a seal to this acquisition of knowledge. There follows Iachimo's description of Imogen's bedchamber—a description carrying extraordinary evocative power (in many ways resembling Enobarbus' in *Antony and Cleopatra*), which recalls in detail all the "particulars" of the room's decoration and emphasizes the naturalness of its artistic quality ("the cutter / was as another Nature").

Posthumus rightly doubts the forensic value of the recalled "circumstances"; Iachimo, he says, could well have learned all this indirectly. The Italian thus produces the bracelet that he had taken off Imogen's arm while she was sleeping. This is the first "corporal sign" to be displayed, and Posthumus immediately gives in to the evidence: "Let there be no honour / Where there is beauty: truth, where semblance: love, / Where there's another man" (2.4.108–10). But his Roman host, Philario, restrains emotion with logic: what holds forensic weight is not the sign itself but the context surrounding it. Perhaps Imogen has lost the bracelet, perhaps a bribed servant stole it. Iachimo begins to swear; Posthumus is already emotionally defeated. But the Italian presents a last "corporal sign" to bring his diabolical logic to its conclusion and to deal a mortal blow to his adversary's psyche: "If you seek / For further satisfying, under her breast / (Worthy her pressing) lies a mole, right proud / Of that most delicate lodging. By my life, / I kiss'd it, and it gave me present hunger / To feed again, though full. You do remember / This stain upon her?" Posthumus' response brings the discussion to a close: "Ay, and it doth confirm / Another stain, as big as hell can hold, / Were there no more but it" (2.4.133–41).

Cymbeline, however, manages to emerge from these two tragic, ignorance-generated abysses (Imogen's, in being overwhelmed by Cloten's headless corpse, and Posthumus', into which he is plummeted by Iachimo's logic) and to pursue its course as romance. Disguised as Fidele, Imogen returns to life from the death she experienced, and entrusts her survival to the flux of circumstance and to the irresistible attraction that her goodness, humility, and loyalty exert on all who meet her. Posthumus' journey is longer and more complex, but it too passes through death. His repentance begins with the finding of the "bloody cloth" that declares to him that Imogen's murder, which he had entrusted to Pisanio, has taken place. This "sign" of death converts him to a new kind of knowledge and openness: to the recognition of the will of the gods. Similarly, and immediately following this, "the heaviness and guilt" within Iachimo's bosom bring to repentance even *Cymbeline's* Iago (5.2).

But Posthumus goes further: he actively seeks death in battle, judging this to be his only chance for redemption, and dedicating it to the memory of Imogen. Later, in the great prison scene, another kind of conscious possibility makes way in him, that of offering his life to the gods in atonement, as "render" for freedom. In a lofty soliloquy, Posthumus repents of having ordered Imogen's death; he also examines his own conscience, asks if repentance is enough, entrusts himself to divine mercy, recognizes, if obliquely, that he is made in the image of the good gods, and ends by invoking the name of his beloved:

> Most welcome bondage; for thou art a way,
> I think to liberty: yet am I better
> Than one that's sick o' th' gout, since he had rather
> Groan so in perpetuity than be cur'd
> By th' sure physician, Death; who is the key
> T' unbar these locks. My conscience, thou art fetter'd

More than my shanks and wrists: you good gods, give me
The penitent instrument to pick that bolt,
Then free for ever. Is't enough I am sorry?
So children temporal fathers do appease;
Gods are more full of mercy. Must I repent,
I cannot do it better than in gyves,
Desir'd more than constrain'd: to satisfy,
If of my freedom 'tis the mainport, take
No stricter render of me than my all.
I know you are more clement than vile men,
Who of their broken debtors take a third,
A sixth, a tenth, letting them thrive again
On their abatement; that's not my desire.
For Imogen's dear life take mine, and though
'Tis not so dear, yet 'tis a life; you coin'd it:
'Tween man and man they weight not every stamp;
Though light, take pieces for the figure's sake:
You rather, mine being yours: and so, great powers,
If you will take this audit, take this life,
And cancel these cold bonds. O Imogen,
I'll speak to thee in silence.

(5.4.3–29)

Then, after the apparitions of his parents and brothers, and the finding of the tablet that contains the secret of his past and the mysterious prophecy of his future, Posthumus finds himself, as had happened earlier to Imogen, at the foundational level of material knowledge: "'Tis still a dream: or else such stuff as madmen / Tongue, and brain not: either both, or nothing, / Or senseless speaking, or a speaking such / As sense cannot untie. / Be what it is, / The action of my life is like it, which / I'll keep, if but for sympathy" (5.4.144–51). And, there arises in him a wisdom that transcends death. In responding to the jailer who, playing on the imminence of execution, wants to place before him the unknowability of a human being's last journey—"for, look you, sir, you know not which way you shall go"—Posthumus simply says: "Yes, indeed do I, fellow." The jailer insists, echoing Hamlet's "to be or not to be": "and how you shall speed in your journey's end, I think you'll never return to tell on." To which Posthumus responds with a *sophia* that recalls that reached by Socrates and Hamlet himself before death: "I tell thee, fellow, there are none want eyes to direct them the way I am going, but such as wink, and will not use them" (5.4.183–88).

WE THUS REACH the climactic scene of the play, that of recognition (5.5), which, in order to untie all the knots in the plot, articulates itself over almost four hundred lines, entailing sixteen successive moments of revelation. This extraordinary sequence brings all of the principal characters on stage after the end of the battle in which the heroism of Belarius, Guiderius, Arviragus, and Posthumus has brought the Britons victory over the Romans. The scene proceeds as follows:

1. Cornelius, the physician, announces to Cymbeline that the queen is dead and reveals her evil nature; the king repents of his "folly" towards Imogen.
2. Instinctively, Cymbeline feels great "paternal" affection toward Fidele.
3. Imogen sees Posthumus' ring on Iachimo's finger and declares that her name is Fidele.
4. Belarius, Guiderius, and Arviragus suspect that "their" Fidele has "revived from death."
5. Pisanio recognizes Imogen in Fidele.
6. Interrogated by Cymbeline on Fidele's request, Iachimo confesses, with elaborate narrative suspense, his deceitfulness in the bet with Posthumus.
7. Infuriated, Posthumus reveals himself and lashes out against himself for having ordered Imogen's death.
8. Fidele tries to calm him but is stricken senseless to the ground by Posthumus. Pisanio exclaims that Fidele is Imogen.
9. Imogen recognizes Pisanio and curses him for having given her the poison. Pisanio reveals that he had received the potion from the queen. Cornelius confirms.
10. Belarius, Guiderius, and Arviragus recognize Fidele.
11. Husband and wife, father and daughter are finally reunited.

12. Pisanio uncovers Cloten's evil plans against Imogen and Posthumus, and Guiderius confesses to having killed him.

13. Cymbeline sentences Guiderius to death but is stopped by Belarius, who proclaims his true identity and reveals that the two young mountain dwellers are in truth his own two sons, Arviragus and Guiderius, and produces evidence to prove it.

14. Cymbeline likens himself to a mother who has given birth to three children. Imogen, Arviragus, and Guiderius recognize themselves as siblings.

15. Cymbeline, who midway through the scene had already felt the world spin around him, asks himself when he will come to know all the "circumstantial branches" of the story.

16. Posthumus reveals himself to be the poor soldier who had valiantly helped Belarius, Guiderius, and Arviragus in the recent battle. Iachimo confirms this and also returns both ring and bracelet. Posthumus spares him. Cymbeline, learning from his son-in-law, forgives everyone and proclaims peace.

Grand in its extension, such orchestration implies a true philosophy of recognition—the recognition that, here, represents the crowning and sublimation of existence in and through goodness, and functions both as a passage from ignorance to knowledge and as a new, more profound, and more vital trajectory of knowledge already possessed. So, while Cymbeline discovers his own sons, Guiderius and Arviragus, in Polydore and Cadwal, he rediscovers Imogen and comprehends the truth about himself. Similarly, Posthumus reexamines his failings and recognizes in Imogen that purest faithfulness which he already knew, but which he allowed himself to be tricked into denying. Guiderius and Arviragus find a sister and understand anew the love they had instinctively felt towards Fidele. A new light shines on existence, as Cymbeline himself declares. Knowledge is not an abstract entity but concerns the flesh and the heart of human beings and, *therefore*, the whole universe. It is no coincidence that, with infinite astonishment, the king should employ both a familial and a cosmic image to describe this moment: he first compares himself to a mother who gives birth to three children, and then immediately sees Guiderius and Arviragus as lords who are able to take possession again of the celestial spheres after their strange, extraordinary, and abnormal deviations from their orbits (5.2.369–70).

Recognition is also artistic achievement, a theatrical exploit realized through inescapable logical concatenation and the inexorable surprises that constitute its most salient moments. Recognition allows the characters to discover their true identity and the profound relations that tie them to each other, and it allows the audience to rediscover the most intimate motives animating the story: traversing the story again in the recognition scene, the audience tastes, in wonder at its artistic construction, the unfolding of the truth. Shakespeare is so conscious of this that he has Cymbeline himself ask a series of questions regarding those parts of the story still obscure to him, thereby expressing his own astonishment and, as a reflection of this, generating that of the audience. Artistic self-awareness thus reaches out its hand to the self-awareness of the audience, and recognition on stage becomes recognition in the theatre:

> O rare instinct!
> When shall I hear all through? This fierce abridgement
> Hath to it circumstantial branches, which
> Distinction should be rich in. Where? how liv'd you?
> And when came you to serve our Roman captive?
> How parted with your brothers? how first met them?
> Why fled you from the court? and whither? These,
> And your three motives to the battle, with
> I know not how much more, should be demanded
> And all the other by-dependances,
> From chance to chance. But nor the time nor place
> Will serve our long inter'gatories. See,
> Posthumus anchors upon Imogen:
> And she (like harmless lightning) throws her eye
> On him: her brothers, me: her master hitting
> Each object with a joy: the counterchange
> Is severally in all.
>
> (5.5.382–98)

Cymbeline feels, in past events, in the moment (*kairós*) he is living, and in himself, the presence of a higher inspiration and "instinct." In his eyes a universal harmony is composed out of light. Imogen is the anchor of everything, the hinge on which it all turns. Now, truly, she is divineness. And fully so: no longer disguised as a boy, she is seen as a woman. It is she who initiates the penetrating exchange of gazes. It is she who turns her eyes on Posthumus "like harmless lightning," in devotion, in love, and in protection. From her that gaze is silently extended (and silence, here, is the dumbfoundedness of love and wonderful sign of union) to her brothers, Guiderius and Arviragus, who turn their eyes to Cymbeline. And now even Posthumus—he too revived, and once again "master" of Imogen—hits "each object with a joy." Now, "the counterchange / Is severally in all," a reciprocal exchange between all involved. This is the harmony that comes after rebirth, when a light that is "a joy" spreads itself over everything. In other words, we are here presented with a resurrection *in the flesh,* giving body to the cosmos' splendor, shining in true Transfiguration.

INDEED, PART OF this complex recognition scene consists in finally having to admit that in *Cymbeline* individual existence and ethics are inextricably tied to the various knots in the plot and to the presence of the transcendent in human life. The theme of death and rebirth dominates the whole play. It is accompanied by constant discussion (sometimes ironic and comic, but more frequently dolorous) of the vices and virtues of human beings; and it is also inserted into a broader debate concerning justice and, in particular, *divine* justice.

When they appear to him in his sleep, the ghosts of Posthumus' parents and brothers raise up an outright song of rebellion against Jupiter, accusing him of having treated the innocent unjustly and threatening even to bring their case before the supreme court of the gods, the "shining synod." This is a radical act of contestation versus divine injustice, like Job's, and could be interpreted as extending to *Cymbeline*'s story as a whole, in which Imogen is unjustly accused and persecuted and Belarius unjustly banished. Jupiter's response comes in the theophany when he descends from heaven, riding his eagle amid thunder and lightning (the pagan equivalent of the whirlwind out of which God speaks to Job). He firmly defines the boundary between the human and the divine, and then speaks the law that governs the unfathomable justice and the secret, providential *caritas* of the divine: "Be not with mortal accidents opprest, / No care of yours it is, you know 'tis ours. / Whom best I love I cross; to make my gift, / The more delay'd, delighted. Be content, / Your low-laid son our godhead will uplift" (5.4.99–103).

What we are presented with here is not a mere traditional *deus ex machina;* rather, it is a richly articulated theodicy. "Mortal accidents" are exclusively in the purview of the divine; human beings should not be anguished by them. "Whom best I love, I crucify," Jupiter seems to say through the use of the word "cross," thereby offering the theological key to the interpretation of the play: happiness can be obtained only after great, painful trials, and it is in any case the free gift of God, who delays in giving it so that human beings might all the more be delighted by it.

Finally, Jupiter leaves behind, in the material world, a physical sign of transcendence, a clue to the unfolding of events that he has announced: the tablet (Posthumus initially calls it a "book") with the prophetic inscription concerning Posthumus' future as well as that of the whole of Britain. As Posthumus observes, this at first appears to be "senseless speaking, or a speaking such / As sense cannot untie." Yet he recognizes immediately that "the action of my life is like it"; and, indeed, the vision witnessed in his sleep unveils to him, indirectly and mysteriously, a knowledge of the "way" beyond death that he will soon glimpse in his dialogue with the jailer.

This vision is, after all, complementary to that of the Roman soothsayer before the battle. Indeed, the play closes with a double act of interpretation, through which both visions are once and for all tied to each other and to the unfolding of history and of the lives of individual humans. And, in words that impart theological significance to *Cymbeline* as a whole and transform the soothsayer into a genuine prophet, the latter recognizes that "the fingers of the powers above do tune / The harmony of this peace" (5.5.467–68). Thus we find prophecy and oracle juxtaposed and integrated—"accomplished"—in being stated once again by the soothsayer near the very final lines of the play:

When as a lion's whelp shall, to himself unknown, without seeking find, and be embrac'd by a piece of tender air: and when from a stately cedar shall be lopp'd branches, which, being dead many years, shall after revive, be jointed to the old stock, and freshly grow, then shall Posthumus end his miseries, Britain be fortunate, and flourish in peace and plenty. (5.5.437–43)

The soothsayer continues:

> For the Roman Eagle,
> From south to west on wing soaring aloft,
> Lessen'd herself and in the beams o' the sun
> So vanish'd; which foreshadow'd our princely eagle,
> Th' imperial Caesar, should again unite
> His favour with the radiant Cymbeline,
> Which shines here in the west.
>
> (5.5.471–77)

Cymbeline, the center of both oracle and prophecy, is a "stately cedar" and "radiant" sun shining on the horizon of history. "Jointed" anew on the old tree, the "branches" of familial bonds revive. Not only Posthumus, whom the soothsayer calls *Leo-natus,* but the whole of *Britannia felix* is embraced by a sweet air: *mollis aer, mulier,* divineness no longer disguised as a boy but embracing all with the aura of a woman—Imogen.

Shakespeare, then, believes in repentance and forgiveness, in divineness, and in the *hope* of immanent transcendence—in fact, in divineness *as* that hope, in our most intimate earthly affections, in the flesh that is the shadow of the beyond. In his last plays, death seems to be for him not an ending but a passage, perhaps even a beginning. He structures human affairs according to the ancient rules of romance and of the marvelous; with intricate and surprising plots he provides a logical explanation for chance and fortune, normally unknowable to us. He presents us[3] with their possible orientation towards salvation.

CHAPTER 5

Resurrection

It is required

You do awake your faith.

The Winter's Tale is governed by an unstoppable imagination, which seems to mock any kind of coherence, be it spatial, chronological, mythical, or even fantastic. Bohemia is on the coast, and on its shores there lurks a murderous bear, which the audience sees on stage. The time in which the play is set is that of classical antiquity, and a prominent role is thus played by an oracle of Apollo arriving from Delphos (neither Delphi nor Delos). Yet Polixenes, King of Bohemia, does not want his name to be associated with that of Judas, who betrayed Jesus, "the Best." His son, Florizel, seems to know well the metamorphoses of the gods; yet his beloved Perdita compares his acting to that of "Whitsun pastorals," the medieval "mysteries" still in vogue in Shakespeare's day. Leontes, king of Sicily, mentions Dame Pertelote, the hen protagonist of the medieval animal epic and of one of Chaucer's tales; yet his wife, Hermione, says that she is daughter of the emperor of Russia.

Moreover, a thief in *The Winter's Tale* named Autolycus claims that he is "littered under Mercury," like Autolycus, son of Hermes and grandfather of Odysseus. Yet in the same scene, a shepherd clown states that the singers are ready for the feast, "most of them means and basses, but one Puritan amongst them, and he sings psalms to hornpipes." Finally, at the end of the play, in a "gallery" that one pictures in the style of the Renaissance, there appears a statue: it is said that this was made by Giulio Romano, who was a distinguished disciple of Raphael and the painter of wondrous frescoes in Mantua, yet never a sculptor (5.2.94–98).[1]

The Winter's Tale is also, explicitly and in its design, one of those "old tales" that Lear and Cordelia would have told each other in prison had they lived long enough to do so. This is defined internally by the play itself, issuing from its plot as the movement of a symphony issues from the first statement of its theme. Indeed, early in the play, Hermione asks her son Mamillius to "tell's a tale," and he decides that "a sad tale's best for winter" (2.1.22–25). Later, the gentlemen who recount the story of Perdita twice call it an "old tale" and specify that it "will have matter to rehearse though credit be asleep and not an ear open" (5.2.28, 61–62). Finally, in the last scene of the play, Paulina declares to Polixenes that if anyone were to say that Hermione lives, he would be "hooted at" for telling "an old tale" (5.3.117). *The Winter's Tale* is precisely that. And it all begins with Leontes' furious jealousy.

Leontes, king of Sicily, is hosting Polixenes, king of Bohemia. The two are dear childhood friends, and Leontes wishes Polixenes could stay with him a while longer, even though matters of state require his friend to return to his own kingdom. To convince him to stay, Leontes has Hermione speak to him. The conversations between Polixenes and Hermione, however, unleash in Leontes a jealousy even more furious than Othello's. Suspicion is itself fatal, and Leontes feels his understanding has been irreparably infected:

> Alack, for lesser knowledge! how accurs'd
> In being so blest! There may be in the cup
> A spider steep'd, and one may drink, depart,
> And yet partake no venom (for his knowledge
> Is not infected): but if one present

Th' abhorr'd ingredient to his eye, make known
How he hath drunk, he cracks his gorge, his sides,
With violent hefts. I have drunk, and seen the spider.
(2.1.38–45)

We are thus presented with a compelling picture of the sickly gift of the knowledge of evil. And we immediately find that, inevitably, this in turn produces yet more evil. Leontes would have his friend poisoned, but, having been warned by Camillo, Polixenes quietly leaves for Bohemia. Camillo too escapes. Leontes, suspecting that the baby girl whom Hermione has given him is in fact Polixenes', orders the loyal Antigonus to take the child "To some remote and desert place, quite out / Of our dominions; and that there thou leave it / (Without more mercy) to its own protection / And favour of the climate." He then puts his wife on trial, naturally finding her guilty, even though he has no evidence against her and the oracle from Delphos proclaims her innocence. Mamillius, son of Leontes and Hermione, dies out of anguish over his mother's fate. Hermione faints, and Leontes moves from the evil infection of his own understanding to repentance for what he has done, and to the intention to atone for his sin:

> Apollo, pardon
> My great profaneness 'gainst thine Oracle!
> I'll reconcile me to Polixenes,
> New woo my queen, recall the good Camillo,
> Whom I proclaim a man of truth, of mercy.
(3.2.151–55)

The king's repentance, however, does not prevent the plot from thickening. Paulina, loyal handmaid to Hermione, soon announces that the queen is dead. Leontes vows to visit daily his wife's and his son's tomb. Antigonus (Paulina's husband) leaves by sea with the little girl, but his vessel is shipwrecked—another shipwreck!—on the coast of Bohemia, where Antigonus is killed by a bear.[2] The infant, who had been named Perdita by her mother, is found by a local shepherd together with a casket containing gold, a mantle, and letters about her identity. Antigonus' corpse and the bundle enveloping the little girl are discovered at the same time: "things dying" and "things new-born" are found together on the same shore (3.3.108–10),[3] as with life itself.

Time now appears on the scene, playing the role of the chorus. Time, a supreme artist, has the power to upset the laws of nature, to represent things as it pleases, and to render both past and present opaque. It thus propels the play forward sixteen years. *The Winter's Tale* is now colored with the hues of comedy, as the scoundrel Autolycus makes his appearance, and with those of pastoral arts. Perdita, raised by the old shepherd, is by now a beautiful young girl, and Florizel, Polixenes' son, falls in love with her. The king, who knows nothing of this, wants to find out with whom his son is spending his days. He thus goes into the countryside and meets Perdita, who, not knowing who he is, offers him flowers as a sign of welcome.

It is here that the theme of Art, closely tied to those of Nature and Time, compellingly emerges. Polixenes tells Perdita that she is beautiful, while he should be adorned instead "with flowers of winter." The girl replies with an enchanting description of the season's flowers:

> Sir, the year growing ancient,
> Not yet on summer's death nor on the birth
> Of trembling winter, the fairest flower o' th'season
> Are our carnations and streaked gillyvors,
> Which some call nature's bastards: of that kind
> Our rustic garden's barren; and I care not
> To get slips of them.
>
> (4.4.79–85)

When Polixenes asks her in response why she neglects these very flowers, Perdita replies: "For I have heard it said / There is an art which, in their piedness, shares / With great creating nature." The young girl sees art as artificiality since the power of creation, for her, lies with *creating* nature alone. Polixenes offers her a subtle and subtly articulated argument:

> Say there be;
> Yet nature is made better by no mean

But nature makes that mean: so over that art,
Which you say adds to nature, is an art
That nature makes. You see, sweet maid, we marry
A gentler scion to the wildest stock,
And make conceive a bark of baser kind
By bud of nobler race. This is an art
Which does mend nature—change it rather—but
The art itself is nature.

> (4.4.88–97)

The vision of the man coming from the world of civilization, and in particular from the culture of the Renaissance (the debate here echoes Montaigne's famous essay on the Cannibals) contrasts with that of someone who lives in the Golden Age and only trusts in the primordial purity of nature. While she accepts the guest's argument, Perdita refuses to use new grafts, "no more that, were I painted, I would wish / This youth should say 'twere well, and only therefore / Desire to breed by me." Like Marina, Perdita is Spring. She picks flowers for her beloved and imagines herself as Proserpina:

O Proserpina,
For the flowers now that, frighted, thou let'st fall
From Dis's waggon! daffodils,
That come before the swallow dares, and take
The winds of March with beauty; violets, dim,
But sweeter than the lids of Juno's eyes
Or Cytherea's breath; pale primroses,
That die unmarried, ere they can behold
Bright Phoebus in his strength (a malady
Most incident to maids); bold oxlips and
The crown imperial; lilies of all kinds,
The flower-de-luce being one.

> (4.4.116–27)

Florizel, on the other hand, to whom this last observation is directed (and who is himself a flower, as his name declares), holds that all that

Perdita does "betters what is done." According to him, Perdita is the supreme Art: the art of Nature. She is dance, as if she were a wave of the sea; she is movement itself. Her every action is the perfection of the *tode ti,* the Greek term for "thisness," of the individual essence which is universal by virtue of its very individuality. Perdita is in fact the encounter between what is right and the right moment, or *kairós:* "Each your doing, / So singular in each particular, / Crowns what you are doing, in the present deeds, / That all your acts are queens" (4.4.135–46).[4]

The wonder of music, dance, flowers, and spring thus bursts into this tale said to be of winter. Polixenes, however, while recognizing in Perdita "something greater than herself, / too noble for this place," wants at all costs to separate the two youths. They escape to Sicily. Leontes, who has spent sixteen years in contrition and who swears to Paulina that he does not want to marry again, welcomes them into his palace as soon as he finds out that Florizel is the son of his friend Polixenes. He does not, however, know who is the young girl who accompanies Florizel.

The first scene of recognition does not occur on stage. It is narrated together with the other parts of the plot, which have so far remained obscure to those who witnessed it, like an "old tale," and with the dream-like pace of fairy tales. One of the gentlemen recounts how the bundle that had enveloped the little girl was opened. Another gentleman continues the story, as he puts it, with a "broken delivery":

> I make a broken delivery of the business; but the changes I perceived in the king and Camillo were very notes of admiration: they seemed almost, with staring on one another, to tear the cases of their eyes: there was speech in their dumbness, language in their very gesture; they looked as they had heard of a world ransomed, or one destroyed: a notable passion of wonder appeared in them; but the wisest beholder, that knew no more but seeing, could not say if th' importance were joy or sorrow; but in the extremity of the one it must needs be. (5.2.9–19)

A world destroyed, a world ransomed: the formula, similar to the "things dying" and "things new-born" of sixteen years earlier, substitutes for a straightforward sequential contrast an only apparent alternative ("a world ransomed, *or* one destroyed"), which in fact reveals itself as a paradoxical identity. We are presented with rebirth: that which dies is saved and comes back to life. This is the play's first announcement and foreshadowing of resurrection: "What you sow does not come to life unless it dies," writes the apostle Paul in his great discourse on the resurrection from the dead (1 Cor. 15:36). It is a miracle that produces a "passion of wonder," wonder without end.

A third gentleman picks up the tale from where the second leaves off. He lists the "proofs" that were found in Perdita's casket: the letters with Antigonus' handwriting, Hermione's mantle with her jewel pinned on its neck, and finally the "majesty" of the infant and her resemblance to her mother. The third gentleman then tells of the meeting between the two kings (the joy of one "crowning" that of the other), the deep emotion felt by the two of them at finding their children anew, and Leontes' cries invoking Hermione. He tells the story of Antigonus' shipwreck and of his brutal end in the bear's mouth. In short, he tells *The Winter's Tale*, this "old tale" originally invented for a dark and cold season but which now enters spring. The plot itself of the play here becomes art: after its being enacted on stage, it is now recreated through words alone and rendered both remote and compelling, enriched and simplified, stupefied and stupefying.

At the end of his story, the third gentleman pauses on a specific detail: in that same meeting between the two kings, Perdita is told the story of her mother's death, to which she responds by "bleeding" tears. She decides to go and see Hermione's statue, kept by Paulina in her palace:

> No: the Princess, hearing of her mother's statue, which is in the keeping of Paulina—a piece many years in doing and now newly performed by that rare Italian master, Julio Romano, who, had he himself eternity and could put breath into his work, would beguile Nature of her custom, so perfectly he is her ape: he so near to Hermione hath done Hermione, that they say one would speak to her and stand in hope of answer. Thither with all greediness of affection are they gone, and there they intend to sup. (5.2.92–100)

Here, once again, is Art. This time, however, we are not dealing with grafting but with sculpture, and specifically with a precious work of the Italian Renaissance. The statue is the creation of the brilliant architect and fantastic painter who built and decorated the Palazzo Te in Mantua; an artist who, as the third gentleman himself says, would, if eternal, be the Creator himself. The newly finished work is such a perfect copy—a *mimesis*—of the original (of Hermione) that it makes one think that Art wins over Nature, that Life is more alive than the life that was. The three gentlemen are convinced that absence from the events that will follow would mean losing the chance of gaining "knowledge" of the "grace" that will newly reveal itself there with "every wink of an eye." They thus set off for Paulina's palace.

AND THUS BEGINS the great scene, with all the protagonists present. This is now no longer a tale; it is both reality and theatre. We are in an actual "gallery," full of "singularities," a private Cinquecento museum. Suddenly, Paulina draws a curtain and reveals the statue. We thus behold a "life as lively mock'd as ever / still sleep mock'd death." Whether it be sleep or death, *The Winter's Tale* never explicitly says, but the unveiling of the statue produces total silence in those present, indicating wonder without end. "I like your silence," Paulina says, "it the more shows off / Your wonder." She seems to be thinking here of Aristotle at the beginning of his *Poetics,* where he declares, in speaking of the pleasure that human beings feel in seeing images imitating figures, that the moment in which we recognize that "this is that" (that is, that the image corresponds to the figure) is supreme (4.1448b4–6).

With unparalleled slowness and in stages, recognition and resurrection now begin. Leontes exclaims that the imitation of Hermione is perfect: "she was as tender / As infancy and grace," and the stone now is "loved." And yet, the statue has wrinkles, which his wife did not have when she died. "So much the more our carver's excellence," Paulina replies, "which lets go by some sixteen years, and makes her / as she lived now." Art thus imagines Time, reads life through it, imitates Nature. It also transcends them, however, concentrating into a sculpture what in life was subject to death. Thus it is that Leontes finds in the statue the "life of majesty" that he had recognized in Hermione when he was courting her, as well as a "magic" that awakens memory and repentance. Thus it is that Perdita would want to kneel before her mother's statue, seek from it a blessing, take its hand to kiss. Meanwhile, asking for forgiveness, Leontes relives his pain, and Polixenes, ready to share the suffering of the other, offers to take it upon himself, thus reaching genuine compassion.

Paulina, who often during the scene threatens to close the curtain, invites those assembled to *patience,* saying that the work is only just finished, the colors not yet dry. But Art enchants: it seems that the statue breathes, that its veins truly have blood in them, and "the very life seems warm upon her lip." "No longer shall you gaze on 't," Paulina says, "lest your fancy / May think anon it moves." But Leontes is won over by the statue: "Let be, let be!" he exclaims, "Would I were dead, but that methinks already— / What was he that did make it?" He observes that "the fixture of her eye has motion in 't / As we are mock'd with art"— the "as," here, drawing a strong and richly ambiguous connection between the apparent movement of the eye and the illusion of art. Leontes indeed wavers between ecstasy and an awareness of art's illusion. Once again, Paulina declares that she will close the curtain, otherwise the king will think the statue is alive. But Leontes declares himself ready to abandon worldly sense and wisdom to embrace the pleasure of the present "madness." He asks again: "What fine chisel / Could ever yet cut breath?" And, finally, he wants to kiss the statue.

Paulina holds him back: "the ruddiness upon her lip is wet," it would be ruined by the kiss. She then offers to close the curtain. But Leontes does not agree— "No: not these twenty years"—so Paulina asks the king and the others present to prepare themselves for even greater amazement. She will make the statue move, descend from its pedestal, and take the hand of the king, who is by this point open to any miracle. Paulina now requires—this is a crucial moment—the birth of *faith:* "it is requir'd / You do awake your faith." She then warns all those who think that what she is about to do is illicit to leave the chapel. Finally, she pronounces a solemn command and invokes music: may it strike and awake the statue. *This* is the time, the *kairós,* the right moment. Let the stone move and come close.

Music, awake her; strike!
'Tis time; descend; be stone no more; approach;
Strike all that look upon with marvel. Come!
I'll fill your grave up: stir, nay, come away,
Bequeath to death your numbness; for from him
Dear life redeems you.

(5.3.98–103)

The tomb in effect is now empty, like Jesus of Nazareth's after three days. Life rescues, *redeems:* from death and its dumbness. The statue's every action, Paulina says, will be "holy." The language is sacred: Shakespeare certainly does not use a verb such as "redeem" by accident, especially in a scene like this one. It is said of Christ that he "abolished death and brought life and immortality to light through the gospel" (2 Tim. 1:10). Yet it is not the resurrection of Jesus that Hermione's coming back to life brings to mind. It echoes, rather, the story of Lazarus as told by John (11:1–44).[5] Paulina's commands—"descend," "approach"—have the force of "Lazarus, come forth!" and her request for faith is similar to that made by Jesus to Martha after he declares to her, "Thy brother shall rise again," and she replies, "I know that he shall rise again in the resurrection at the last day." Jesus' response first proclaims one of the central truths of John's Gospel and then ends with the question that interests us here: "I am the resurrection, and the life: he that believeth in me, though he were dead, yet shall he live: and whosoever liveth and believeth in me shall never die. Believest thou this?"

The Gospel we are reading here, however, is that according to Shakespeare, who leaves all options open. Hermione moves; "Hermione comes down," the stage directions read. "O, she's warm!" Leontes exclaims, "If this be magic, let it be an art / Lawful as eating." This is a strange Easter morning, in which a sculpted image comes back to life. This rebirth has all the appearance of a Renaissance, of the flourishing anew of culture and, indeed, of art: Giulio Romano has not been evoked by chance. Hermione now holds on to Leontes, embraces him, and thus forgives him, suffers with him, rejoices with him. She is asked to speak, to reveal where she has lived or how she has managed to escape death: human questions that would like to penetrate the mystery or reduce everything to fiction. Paulina responds with a paradox: "That she is living, / Were it but told you, should be hooted at / Like an old tale: but it appears she lives" (5.3.115–17). Perhaps it is an "old tale," like those that *should* make one smile (although Lear and Cordelia, "God's spies," would smile out of joy); *but*, it is obvious (obvious to the senses) that Hermione is, now, living.

And what if the old tale were a parable? Paulina shows Hermione her recovered daughter. And, finally, Hermione speaks: she invokes the grace of the gods upon Perdita and asks *her* to tell the story of her salvation, her life, her being found. As for herself, she simply says that, in the hope of seeing her daughter alive again, she "preserved" herself "to see the issue." Preserved in death, with body intact? Or preserved in life? These are the questions we ask ourselves together with Leontes, who soon after wants to know *how:* "for I saw her, / As I thought, dead; and have in vain said many / A prayer upon her grave" (5.3.139–41). Hamlet, who continues to entertain doubts about the ghost, would probably say the same thing. And joining company with him would be the apostle Thomas, who, when Jesus announces to his disciples that Lazarus is dead, accepts the sad fact—"Let us also go, that we may die with him"— and, later, doubts his Master's resurrection.

So, what is more plausible, an "old tale" or a statue that comes to life? For this is the option that Shakespeare gives us. We are called to decide between two alternative fictions: that of life miraculously preserving itself through time and adversity, and that of art, which, in its verisimilitude, brings what is dead back to life. To collapse the two into one, and to say that Hermione was never dead and only comes back to life in the form of a statue because Paulina wants to play an astonishing trick, is reasonable. It is *too* reasonable, for a scene and a play that offer no clarity in this regard; and it is too reasonable for life, and for death, which do not offer explanations.

Moreover, if we can believe, through the "suspension of disbelief" that Coleridge says is necessary for the fruition of art, that a statue can perfectly imitate a real person—if, that is to say, we can believe in the miracle of art—then Shakespeare would seem to suggest that we can also believe in the resurrection of the dead, the mystery and miracle preached by Christianity, without which, as Paul says, "is our preaching vain, and your faith is also vain."[6] Shakespeare seems to be telling us that all that is necessary for faith is suspension of disbelief. This would be sensational good news, complementing and updating our modern sensibility with that of the New Testament and of Dante's *Divine Comedy*, in which faith is "the assurance of things hoped for, the conviction of things not seen" (Heb. 11:1): "sustanza di cose sperate / ed argomento de le non parventi" (*Par.* 24.64–65).

Marina, Thaisa, Perdita, Hermione: these parables preach, in feminine mode (and therefore in terms even more revolutionary than the Gospels themselves), the resurrection of the flesh; not in the otherworld or on the Last Day but here, now, in a world that is ours but also new, in a time that is human yet also deferred (Hermione's sixteen years, Marina's whole life). In the Nicene Creed, common to all Christians, this is called "vita *venturi saeculi*," the life of the world to come. In Shakespeare's Gospels such a resurrection is announced on the basis of the most human kinds of affection, on love that is apparently ordinary and banal yet is the most profound: that between husband and wife, between fathers, mothers, and children. As the First Letter of John declares, "We know that we have passed from death unto life, because we love the brethren. He that loveth not his brother abideth in death" (3:14).

It is perhaps worth recalling here the extraordinary "Amen" that, in *Paradiso* 14, Dante has the blessed souls of the wise exhale as soon as Solomon—who had been speaking with a voice similar to Gabriel's to Mary at the Annunciation—ends his explanation regarding the increasing brightness of the *flesh* after the resurrection. That "Amen," Dante says, is a manifestation of the desire of the blessed—who are now, simply, light—to regain their "dead bodies." He then adds, quite unexpectedly, and as if he were thinking of Shakespeare's romances, that such desire is shown "forse non pur per lor, ma per le mamme, / per li padri e per li altri che fuor cari / anzi che fosser sempiterne fiamme" (*Par.* 14.61–66): not perhaps for themselves alone, but for their mothers, for their fathers, and for the others who were dear before they became eternal flames.

But let us try to be rational. If I had to express the problem posed by the end of *The Winter's Tale* in logical terms, I would put it as follows.

Four interpretations are possible: (1) The whole thing is a lie, mere fiction. Hermione has always been alive, and here does little else than resume her life at court, joining Leontes and Perdita again after sixteen years. After all, she herself says that she "preserved" herself. (2) What Paulina performs is magic. Indeed, she worries that those who are present might take it as such. (3) We are dealing here with the mystery of art, of the *perfect* imitation of reality. In fact, all of *The Winter's Tale* addresses this question; and in the last scene the miracle and trick of artistic mimesis are constantly emphasized. (4) The fundamental aspect of the final scene of the play is resurrection (of the flesh). Indeed, Paulina specifically says, "I'll fill your grave up."

All four interpretations are legitimate (skeptical moderns will choose almost without hesitation between the first, which will be preferred by a majority of spectators,[7] and the third, completely neglecting the second and the fourth). Regarding the first, however, one would have to account for the fact that Leontes firmly holds that he has seen Hermione dead and prayed at her tomb. Moreover, why would Shakespeare invent such an elaborate scene, which is not strictly necessary to the resolution of the plot? He could have ended the play with a scene like Marina's and Pericles' or Pericles' and Thaisa's, without the need for the statue—without, that is, bringing art into play and using the music that Paulina employs to awaken Hermione. Regarding the second, one would then have to note Paulina's statement that she has *not* been "assisted / By wicked powers" and that her actions are not "unlawful." Concerning the third, one should at least observe that no art can provide an imitation of nature so perfect as to make it seem that a statue breathes ("What fine chisel / Could ever yet cut breath?" Leontes asks). Before the work of art we do recognize, as maintained by Aristotle, that "this is that," but we are also aware that it is fiction, imitation. Finally, about the fourth possibility, we would have to admit that, strictly speaking, this cannot be an actual resurrection of the flesh, because what comes back to life is a statue, not Hermione's dead body, which after sixteen years would presumably be putrefied, unless it had somehow been "preserved" intact.

My answer is the following. Each of the four interpretations could be easily and rationally dismantled by its respective objections. And yet,

Shakespeare's text is able to keep all four in place because to each one it responds with the other three. In other words, the four positions are *inextricable* one from the other. And that is because the mysteries of life, magic, art, and resurrection are *equal*. The important thing is—so the text seems to suggest—that we keep awake our "faith," that we suspend our disbelief in *all* senses, that we remain open *to all four* of the mysteries. It's not much; but this is, indeed, what a work of literature can do to help us be born again to life.

Leontes was furiously jealous, unreasonable, blind, and unjust: he drank and saw the spider. That was his—and our—hell. He then went through the purgatory of a life lived with guilt and of atonement through repentance. Through the invocation of forgiveness comes a "consummation," to cite Hamlet once again, that has all the features of the divine. But such divine fulfillment—or heaven—is rooted in the human, in the most intimate of affections: daughter and wife. Life is earthly, here and now: it is for *this* reason that we are "required" to recognize it, through faith, as magic, masterpiece, miracle.

CHAPTER 6

Epiphany

I might call him

A thing divine

The Tempest brings unusual and complex Good News. In this multiform, metamorphic, and ungraspable play, in which Shakespeare's fantasy moves freely in many directions, there is both the telling of a human gospel and also the staging of something that possesses a sacred aura. Before claiming as much, however, we must read *The Tempest* attentively, listen to its music, imagine its action and its panorama. Its plot (which has no sources) is simple, characterized—for once in Shakespeare's work—by unity of space and time; and it is, indeed, the bearer of good news. In essence, what happens is that a ship en route from Tunis to Naples—carrying Alonso, the king of Naples, his brother Sebastian and his son Ferdinand, Antonio, the usurping duke of Milan, the old counselor Gonzalo, and other courtiers and mariners on board—is shattered by a tempest and wrecked on the coast of a mysterious and enchanted island.

On the island live Prospero, the rightful duke of Milan, his daughter Miranda, the "slave" Caliban, son of the African witch Sycorax, and the spirit Ariel, the only native of the island, whom Sycorax had imprisoned in a tree and whom Prospero had rescued in exchange for his services. Antonio, in agreement with the king of Naples, had snatched the dukedom of Milan from his brother Prospero, who, immersed in his studies, had entrusted its government to him. Prospero and Miranda, as the protagonist reveals to his daughter, had been expelled from Lombardy and entrusted to the waves of the sea on a small vessel, which, by "providence divine," had deposited them on the island.

They survive here thanks to Prospero's great magical art and to Caliban's services. Once they have met, Ferdinand and Miranda fall in love. Prospero is happy about this but pretends to place obstacles between them. Caliban offers his help to Stephano and Trinculo, respectively, the butler and jester to Alonso, to organize a coup against his master. Later, Sebastian and Antonio plot to seize the kingdom of Naples from Alonso. Having undermined such conspiracies, Prospero rejects his magic and reveals himself to the newcomers, asking for restitution of the dukedom and pointing out to everyone Miranda and Ferdinand, now betrothed, playing chess. He then frees Ariel and clearly suggests that he will forgive the repentant Caliban, who will remain the only inhabitant of the island. Prospero, Miranda, and Ferdinand will set sail with the others towards Naples and celebrate the marriage of the two young people. Prospero will then retire to Milan, where, he declares, "every third thought" will be for his grave.

Instead of the recognition scenes of *Pericles, Cymbeline,* and *The Winter's Tale,* we have three marvelous revelation scenes, three true epiphanies: the encounter between Miranda and Ferdinand, Prospero's unveiling of himself before the courtiers of Naples and Milan, and the great scene of Ferdinand and Miranda playing chess. It is on these that I will concentrate. But I will do so following the unfolding of the action, which, like the island itself, is from a thematic point of view a true "maze": full of surprises, mysterious twists, and enigmatic amplifications, accelerations and delays, lyrical and musical expansions, and moments of concentrated rapture.

The tempest that has overwhelmed the Neapolitan ship is immediately revealed as an illusion: it is in fact created by Prospero, who, like the God of the Bible, "commanded and raised the stormy wind, which lifted up the waves of the sea" (Ps. 107:25). The king, duke, lords, and mariners sailing from Tunis to Naples are all safe: "Not a hair perished," Ariel confirms to Prospero, echoing the words of St. Paul in the tempest that throws his ship onto the shores of Malta during the apostle's voyage to Rome (1.2.217; Acts 27:34). While the fake tempest and the fake shipwreck take place, Miranda and her father are in front of the "cell" that is their home. Prospero reassures his daughter, who had suffered with those whom she had seen in distress, that they have been done "no harm," that he himself has "ordered" the tempest "with such provision in my art," and that he has acted for her own good. He then tells her of his brother's betrayal and of the sea voyage with the books that Gonzalo had preserved for him and with her infant self: a "cherubin," smiling, "Infusèd with a fortitude from heaven"; an angel who truly did "preserve" him. The expulsion from Milan is "foul" but, he recognizes, "blessèd" is their arrival on the island. Prospero closes his tale by affirming that it is Fortune (now his "dear lady") that has at present brought his enemies here. He then makes Miranda fall into a deep sleep.

All are safe, Neapolitan and Milanese, but separated and ignorant of each other's fate. Ariel, now that Miranda sleeps, tells Prospero how he staged the tempest, burning as an inexplicable fire in different parts of the ship—"I flamed amazement"—and then how he separated those shipwrecked. On one side of the island is Ferdinand, alone; the mariners are stowed under the hatches, sunken in sleep; while on another side of the island is everyone else. The ship itself is hid "in the deep nook, where once / Thou call'dst me up at midnight to fetch dew / From the still-vex'd Bermoothes" (1.2.227–29).

This is the first extraordinary excess of the play (there is no need for Ariel to add all these details), the first fantastic leap of the many with which *The Tempest* will enchant us: towards the dew of other islands, the Bermudas of the New World constantly vexed by the wind. Prospero, more corporeal, would like the reluctant Ariel to undertake a new task. The spirit, who instead desires his freedom, is reminded by his master how he had drawn him out of the pine tree in which Sycorax had confined him. During the course of their animated discussion, there also emerges the story of the Algerian witch, exiled onto the island with her child in her womb. On Prospero's instructions, Ariel transforms himself into a "nymph of the sea," while father and daughter enter the cell where Caliban is gathering wood for them. There follows a spirited dialogue between the master, who rebukes Caliban for having tried to rape Miranda, Miranda herself, who reminds Caliban how she had taught him language and thought, and the slave, who, as the only native of the island, claims it as his lawful property and declares that the only thing he ever got from learning their language is knowing how to curse. Prospero, threatening him with terrible night cramps, forces Caliban to obey his orders; his master's art, the latter confesses, is so powerful that it would "make a vassal" of Setebos, his mother's god.

> And then take hands;
> Courtsied when you have and kiss'd
> The wild waves whist:
> Foot it featly here and there,
> And sweet spirits bear
> The burthen. Hark, hark!
> > (1.2.374–80)

Ariel then evokes watchdogs barking, "Bow-wow!" and the cock singing at the top of its voice, "Cock-a-diddle-dow!" Before this cascade of enchanted and naturalistic notes Ferdinand is astonished. He asks himself from where the music might be coming, whether in the air or on the earth, concludes that he is certainly following some "god" of the island, and then replies to Ariel's poem with his own:

> Sitting on a bank,
> Weeping again the king my father's wreck,
> This music crept by me upon the waters,
> Allaying both their fury and my passion
> With its sweet air: thence I have follow'd it,
> Or it hath drawn me rather. But 'tis gone.[1]
> > (1.2.392–97)

Instead, the music immediately starts again, with Ariel now echoing the words of Ferdinand and evoking the death by water of his father, suggesting, however, a mysterious metamorphosis of his body into corals and pearls, "Into something rich and strange"; perhaps, we think, something that perishes into intriguing and lasting beauty:

> Full fathom five thy father lies;
> Of his bones are coral made;
> Those are pearls that were his eyes:
> Nothing of him that doth fade,
> But doth suffer a sea-change
> Into something rich and strange.
> Sea-nymphs hourly ring his knell.
> (1.2.399–405)

The song ends with the repeated sound of bells, "Ding-dong." Those who have had the good fortune of listening to the music that Robert Johnson composed for *The Tempest* at the time of its first performances will realize what an irresistible and fascinating attraction these lines already possess on their own terms. A funereal song, slow and *sotto voce*, transforms itself into the murmur of life and then inserts new music into the music (it is Ariel who sings the bell of the nymphs: "Hark, now I hear them: Ding-dong"); this resounding of the small bells confirms the death by water and leads us towards transformation and mystery, as if it were a baptism, and towards the possibility, perhaps, of survival.

Indeed, life now immediately takes over, a new scene budding from the preceding one like a second flower on the stem. Ferdinand is perturbed: the song, he observes, recalls the drowned father; it is no "mortal" thing, or human, "nor no sound that the earth owes." He hears it, now, above him, in the air. But Prospero and Miranda are watching; the father invites the daughter to open her eyes and tell him what she sees "yon." Shakespeare thus unfolds with supreme delicacy and force the first, double, epiphany of the play. Miranda believes the man to be a spirit but immediately notes that he is extremely beautiful—"a brave form"—and that he is looking all around himself. No, not a spirit, the father replies, "it eats and sleeps and hath such senses / As we have, such." Ferdinand has escaped the shipwreck and is wandering in search of his companions, "and but he's something stained / With grief, that beauty's canker, thou mightst call him / A goodly person." The beauty of the first other human being, then, is striking, uniting nobility and goodness: in *kalokagathia,* as in *Pericles,* in *Cymbeline,* and in *The Winter's Tale.* But here it is even stronger because it is primordial. Prospero is condescending; Miranda is astonished and, as her father is quick to notice, already in love. "I might call him / a thing divine," she replies, "for nothing natural / I ever saw so noble." She sees in Ferdinand the beauty and perfection of a god.

Ferdinand reacts in the same way. Like Odysseus before Nausicaa, he believes Miranda to be a goddess, then calls her "wonder" and asks her if she is a "maid." No, not a wonder, is her reply, but yes, certainly a maid. Ferdinand, then, is struck by the fact that she speaks his language and declares himself first among all who speak it, now that his father is dead. Prospero immediately rebukes him, while also noting that, as his spirit actually desired, "At the first sight / they have changed eyes . . . They are both in either's powers." Prospero then promises to free Ariel in two days' time, for having accomplished all this.

Ariel, with the enchantment of his songs, has led Ferdinand to Miranda, as Prospero wished. Might Ariel, with the music, also have instilled love in Ferdinand? Did not his first song invite him to take hands? Be that as it may (and this will be one of the many threads that *The Tempest* will leave hanging loose in the mind), the two young people are now tied. Miranda, who wonders why her father is so rude to the guest, declares this to be the third man she sees and the first for whom she sighs. Ferdinand replies by offering to marry her and make her queen of Naples. The union is perfect: a man and a woman who appear to be gods encounter each other, love each other, promise themselves to each other.

It is as if someone were describing the scene in which Adam and Eve see each other for the first time. To her father, who accuses Ferdinand of being a spy who has arrived on the island to take it from him, Miranda opposes her own faith in the inextricability of goodness and beauty, in *kalokagathia:* "There's nothing ill," she says, "can dwell in such a temple. / If the ill spirit have so fair a house, / Good things will strive to dwell with't." In fact, Prospero wants to reinforce the union between the two and put it to the test: when Ferdinand reacts to the accusation by drawing his sword, he is immediately immobilized by a spell. Miranda's attempt at intercession is blocked by the threat of a rage that one imagines to be like that of Lear towards Cordelia at the moment of the division of the kingdom, and by the reduction—sensible, of course—of Ferdinand to ordinary human proportions: "Thou think'st," Prospero hisses at his daughter, "there is no more such shapes as he, / Having seen but him and Caliban. Foolish wench! / To th' most of men this is a Caliban, / And they to him are angels." Miranda replies with the simple, firm, affirmation of love: "My affections / Are then most humble. I have no ambition / To see a goodlier man." While he is led to imprisonment by Prospero, Ferdinand confirms the same faith on his part: his vigor "as in a dream . . . all bound up," the loss of his father, the threats of Prospero, would all be light burdens if he could, once a day, contemplate "this maid" from his prison.

We behold the happiness of love, its absolute and unfailing and invincible nature, as it already existed between Perdita and Florizel in *The Winter's Tale*. But it is made more intense, intangible, by the astonishment, the joining of goodness and beauty, and the aura of the Beginning that envelops the scene on a remote island, which, as Ferdinand will later say, is "paradise." It is a paradise that Eve has entered first, as a child, as willed by Providence in exile from History, from Milan, and where Adam is thrown by the waves, by the action of Fortune, of Chance outside History, outside Tunis and Naples. And God (in this case, Prospero) watches the action and governs it. It is a double epiphany in which the infinite wonder felt by the protagonists opens and expands their spirit (as well as that of the audience) like an *ekplexis*, a blow that, through their surprise, brings them closer and unites them forever.

THE SECOND ACT transports us to two different parts of the island: first to the bay where King Alonso, Duke Antonio, and their men have reached shore, and then to where Caliban has loaded himself with firewood to deliver to Prospero's cell. They are two mirror-like scenes, in which the main themes are those of power and colonization. In the first, Antonio persuades Sebastian to get rid of his brother Alonso and thus take possession of the kingdom of Naples, as he did in Milan against Prospero. Now that Ferdinand, the legitimate heir, is, as they believe, dead, and now that his sister Claribel has been given in marriage to the King of Tunis, the road to usurpation is clear.

Dominating the conversation are Carthage (Tunis) and Dido, that is, the Virgilian model of the colonization of Africa (and, behind it, the paradigm of Aeneas conquering Italy). To this, however, is opposed the utopia of old Gonzalo, who immediately notes not only that the survivors' clothes are dry, fresh, and bright despite the shipwreck, but most importantly, that on the island on which they were thrown by the tempest the grass is lush and green. In other words, "Here everything is advantageous to life." If, Gonzalo says, this island were his own "plantation" (the term means the right to colonization), he would organize the "commonwealth" in a manner fully opposite to prevailing European practice. There would be no commerce, magistrates, letters, riches, poverty, servitude, contracts, inheritances, boundaries, or working of the land; no metals, corn, wine, oil, armaments, or machinations; abolished would be all work, sovereignty, and private property ("All things in common"). Nature would produce what is necessary—"Without sweat or endeavour"—in this state of being, which Gonzalo himself defines as superior even to the "Golden Age." This is the translation into utopia of the reality of the New World that Montaigne described in his essay *Des Cannibales,* translated into English and read by Shakespeare in John Florio's version.

Gonzalo's dream has no effect and is instead derided by the courtiers, who ready themselves, according to Old World habits, for conspiracy and the elimination of Alonso. Ariel intervenes twice, first to make everyone but the conspirators Antonio and Sebastian fall asleep, and then to wake Alonso again and alert him. The company finally sets off through the "maze" of the island in search of Ferdinand.

But the other side of the coin of Gonzalo's dream is ready for us in the second scene. While Caliban, loaded with firewood under the distant sound of thunder, curses Prospero for his tyranny and the suffering he inflicts on him, the two Neapolitan crew members, first Trinculo and then Stephano, arrive. The encounter between the native, Caliban, and the strangers is modeled on the Commedia dell'Arte, but it is also a satire (amusing, bitter, and truthful) of the encounter between European man and the "other." Caliban mistakes Trinculo for one of Prospero's spirits, and Trinculo takes Caliban to be a stinking fish, a "monster" who has the legs of a man, "an islander that hath lately suffered by a thunderbolt." Stephano, who sings "a very scurvy tune" and has a bottle in his hand, sees in Caliban a devil who "put tricks upon 's with savages and men of Ind"; if he can tame him with wine, he could be worth a fortune in Naples. Stephano and Trinculo recognize each other (a first parody of the epiphany we have just witnessed), and the former gives a drink to Caliban, whom he calls "monster" and "dead moon-calf." And Caliban calls the strangers "fine things": Stephano is the "brave god" before whom he kneels. This is the second parody of the revelation between Ferdinand and Miranda, but most of all it is the staging of the misunderstanding that often characterized the encounters between Europeans and natives in the New World. Caliban, upon the liquor that he declares "not earthly," "celestial," swears to become a faithful subject of Stephano, whom he believes has dropped down from the moon. He adores him and beseeches him to be his god. The two mariners, on the other hand, who believe that the king and courtiers were drowned, consider themselves the lords of the island. They call Caliban an abominable, shallow, weak, poor, perfidious, credulous, drunk, scurvy, and ridiculous monster. Caliban is none of these; the alcohol-induced and abject state into which he has fallen does not prevent his primitive delicacy from pronouncing a commitment to servitude that seems to be a celebration of the innocence, the ingenuous nature, and the simplicity of the "noble savage":

> I prithee, let me bring thee where crabs grow;
> And I with my long nails will dig thee pig-nuts;
> Show thee a jay's nest and instruct thee how
> To snare the nimble marmoset; I'll bring thee
> To clustering filberts and sometimes I'll get thee
> Young scamels from the rock. Wilt thou go with me?
>   (2.2.167–72)

The wine is then the seed of revolt: no more wood loads and plate washing. "'Ban, 'ban, Cacaliban / Has a new master.—Get a new man! / Freedom, high-day! High-day, freedom! Freedom, high-day, freedom!"

This is a beautiful hymn and a sad one, considering who pronounces it, the man to whom it is directed, and the next two centuries of history. There is, however, someone else who drags logs across the island. It is Ferdinand, ordered by Prospero to stockpile thousands of them, but he does this while thinking of Miranda, who "quickens what's dead," and the thought of whom relieves his exhaustion. Miranda, whose father has forbidden her to meet her beloved, disobeys and, while Prospero contemplates the scene unseen, offers to carry the logs herself ("Poor worm," her father comments, "thou art infected"). Ferdinand refuses but asks for her name. The epiphany of the first act resumes intact, as if nothing had happened, at the beginning of the third.

"Miranda," the young woman replies, reprimanding herself for having disobeyed her father. Ferdinand thus launches into a paean for such a name and for the woman who bears it: "Admired Miranda!" he exclaims, "Indeed the top of admiration." In her very being, Miranda bears wonder, the primordial astonishment of the human being before the world, and she is herself the object of wonder, of admiration. Ferdinand confesses to having looked at many other women in the past, and to have been taken by one or another of their virtues. All, however, had some imperfection. But not Miranda; she is "So perfect and so peerless . . . created / of every creature's best." The young woman replies with humility and ardor. She does not know or remember other women, and has never seen men other than him and her own "dear" father, but she wants no companion other than himself: "Nor can imagination form a shape / besides yourself to like of." Miranda is audacious (as Shakespeare's heroines often are) and does not hesitate to reveal her love. When Ferdinand declares to her that from the moment he saw her, his heart flew to her service, the young woman simply asks: "Do you love me?" And when the young man replies with a solemn oath worthy of a traditional lover, she is not able to control herself: "I am a fool / to weep at what I am glad of."

Thanks to Miranda's innocence and deep emotion, the epiphany has become—as Prospero remarks in watching the scene and invoking heavenly grace "On that which breeds between 'em"—an "encounter" of two "most rare" feelings, of affections that are earthly, and therefore precious. Here is the communion of man and woman, of two human beings, and therefore, as Prospero says, "fair." It is Miranda's impulsive behavior that makes this one of the most moving love scenes Shakespeare ever wrote. When Ferdinand asks her why she is crying, the young woman replies with disarming candor: "At mine unworthiness, that dare not offer / What I desire to give, and much less take / What I shall die to want." Then, she banishes cunning and invokes her own simple and "holy" innocence: "I am your wife, if you will marry me. / If not, I'll die your maid." Ferdinand responds with enthusiasm. But it is the feminine heart that has first pronounced the truth, found itself, and revealed itself; the traditional love scene transforms itself into what Hamlet would call a "consummation," the fulfillment of the epiphany begun earlier. Prospero seals it with his words, while the two young people depart from each other and the scene: "So glad of this as they I cannot be, / Who are surprised with all; but my rejoicing / At nothing can be more" (3.1.92–94).

In the meantime, the two conspiracies—against Prospero and against Alonso—continue to take shape, but they are frustrated by Ariel's intervention. Caliban, Stephano, and Trinculo try to reach the cell where they will kill Prospero—as Caliban recommends—after having seized his books, without which "He's but a sot as I am, nor hath not / One spirit to command." Ariel, who is invisible, interposes himself in their dialogue, provoking a quarrel; then, playing a tabor and pipe, he resumes the song they are singing. "This is the tune of our catch," the frightened Trinculo observes, "played by the picture of Nobody." Caliban encourages his companions:

> Be not afeard; the isle is full of noises,
> Sounds and sweet airs, that give delight and hurt not.
> Sometimes a thousand twangling instruments
> Will hum about mine ears, and sometimes voices,
> That, if I then had waked after long sleep,
> Will make me sleep again: and then, in dreaming,

The clouds methought would open and show riches
Ready to drop upon me; that, when I wak'd,
I cried to dream again.

(3.2.133–41)

Even a savage, a monster, can dream and cry in desire on the enchanted island of *The Tempest*, whose landscape is never described, in spite of Ariel's singing of yellow sands, Gonzalo's talk of lush grass and tortuous paths, and the trees that, we imagine, provide the wood that Caliban and Ferdinand load on their shoulders. It is instead a speaking land, a land of sounds, voices, and music, of sweet and innocuous airs, of murmurs, of instruments that vibrate, that give delight and bring sleep. There seems to be nothing between the ground and the clouds that, as Caliban dreams, will open and show riches ready to be rained down, if not the notes "played by the picture of Nobody."

The Neapolitans' march continues, in the meantime, through the "maze" in search of Ferdinand. While Antonio and Sebastian agree to eliminate Alonso during the night, another wonder occurs. A strange and solemn music resounds in the air, and there appear various "spirits, in several strange shapes" who prepare a banquet and, dancing and greeting, invite the king and his men to eat. Prospero is above the scene, invisible. The strangers are dumbstruck and by now are ready to believe the most fantastic tales of travelers to unknown lands, but, famished, they approach the table. However, amid thunder and lightning, Ariel arrives in the shape of a harpy; he flaps his wings and, "with a quaint device," the banquet vanishes. We are reminded of Isaiah's words, "Just as when a hungry person dreams of eating and wakes up still hungry." The words themselves would seem to be directed at the biblical Ariel, that is, Jerusalem, prophesying the Lord's visit "with thunder and earthquake and great noise, with whirlwind and *tempest,* and the flame of a devouring fire" (Isa. 29:8, 6; emphasis mine).[2]

Ariel plays the part of the implacable harpy extremely well: for those whom he calls "three men of sin"—Alonso, Antonio, and Sebastian—destiny, "that hath to instrument this lower world," has prepared the shipwreck on this island, where no human being dwells, because they are unworthy of living among human beings. The harpy, for this reason, has made them mad, and it is useless for them to draw their swords. They are by now too exhausted to raise them, and Ariel and his companions are, on their part, invulnerable. The harpy acts not only on the body and nerves but also on the spirit. Its words are those of conscience, that "deity" which Antonio, earlier, had claimed not to hear, of which he claimed not to know the dwelling place (2.1.271–75). Ariel recalls, indeed, that the Milanese supplanted Prospero, abandoning him and his daughter on the sea, which has now repaid them. It is on account of this foul deed that "the powers" incensed the waters, took his son from Alonso, and now pronounce lingering ruin. For such retributive justice, which punishes the sinner in a manner fitting the sin, there is only one remedy, the harpy maintains: "heart's sorrow / and a clear life ensuing," in other words, repentance and a radical change in their mode of living. With this Christian intimation, Ariel disappears amid the thunder. He has spoken, for Prospero, as the God of the Bible, while disguised as a harpy in a Virgilian scene, with the tone of *Everyman*'s Death.[3] Accompanied by soft music, the spirits reappear, dancing and mocking the bystanders, and take away the table. While Prospero praises Ariel's performance, Alonso reacts, thinking that the waves spoke to him and that the thunder pronounced Prospero's name, denouncing his crime. "Therefore my son i' th' ooze is bedded, and / I'll seek him deeper than e'er plummet sounded, / and with him there lie mudded."

Alonso prefigures death, perhaps suicide. Sebastian and Antonio, inveterate in sin, propose to fight and defeat the "fiends" that have just assailed them. Gonzalo understands that in different ways, the three are "desperate," and it is guilt, "like poison given to work a great time after," that is now biting into their minds. Despair—the absence of hope—is the most serious sin, that which brought Judas to hang himself. The madness in which the three are entangled is this: the impossibility of departing from guilt by means of repentance. Shakespeare has crafted not an allegory but rather an extraordinary spectacle of syncretistic ritual, a shadow of Christian doctrine in para-classical garb. He has composed a scene worthy of Marlowe's *Doctor Faustus*, but, anticipating by two centuries Goethe's *Faust*, he has introduced into it "strange shapes" and a harpy drawn from the *Aeneid*. A mysterious table is prepared for a banquet, almost as if it were Don Giovanni's last supper in Mozart's opera. He then makes it disappear; he inflicts on the sinners the suffering of Tantalus and denies them participation in the miraculous banquet of human and divine communion.

TWO SPECTACLES and an apocalypse await us in the fourth act, which are even more intriguing than the preceding events. Ferdinand has stood the test imposed by Prospero ("strangely," Prospero notes). He now receives, as gift "afore heaven," Miranda, with the injunction, however, not to possess her until "All sanctimonious ceremonies may / With full and holy rite be ministered." Prospero, who wants to present the couple with "some vanity" of his magical art, calls again upon Ariel, who instantly obeys, taking this opportunity to ask his master if he loves him (the reply to the surprising, touching request is "dearly"). He gathers many spirits and, to the sound of soft music, stages a masque, a spectacle fashionable at the courts of the time. It is a mythological performance in which Iris, the many-colored messenger of the gods, the "heavenly bow" and "wat'ry arch" (the rainbow), summons Ceres—goddess, as her name implies, of growth, of fertility, and of harvest—to a meeting with Juno.

We never see, unless by glimpses, the landscape in *The Tempest*, but now we witness the flourishing of Nature, not here, on the wild and deserted island, but in an ideal, Edenic land that is the mythical equivalent of Gonzalo's utopia. We find again Marina's, Perdita's, and Imogen's flowers but accompanied, now, by fruit, by wheat and rye, by grass and flocks, by barley and oats, and by the vineyard. It is a bucolic, pastoral Nature, simply outlined by the words of the goddesses, but no less vivid for it. It is a heavenly but cultivated landscape, where April—Spring—is married to the nymphs and the broom-groves to sea rocks; a total landscape that extends from mountain to plain, to river bank, to the rocky coast where Ceres goes to breathe, to blow her breath of life. This is how Iris invites the goddess of the harvest:

> Ceres, most bounteous lady, thy rich leas
> Of wheat, rye, barley, vetches, oats and pease;
> Thy turfy mountains, where live nibbling sheep,

And flat meads thatch'd with stover, them to keep;
Thy banks with pioned and twilled brims,
Which spongy April at they hest betrims,
To make cold nymphs chaste crowns; and thy broom-groves,
Whose shadow the dismissed bachelor loves,
Being lass-lorn; thy pole-clipt vineyard;
And thy sea-marge, sterile and rocky-hard,
Where thou thyself dost air;—the queen o' th' sky,
Whose wat'ry arch and messenger am I,
Bids thee leave these; and with her sovereign grace,
Here on this grass-plot, in this very place,
To come and sport:—her peacocks fly amain:
Approach, rich Ceres, her to entertain.

                                                    (4.1.60–75)

Ceres gladly accepts, returning praise to Iris—she who with "saffron wings" spreads drops of honey and refreshing showers on Ceres' flowers, she who as "rich scarf to my proud earth" crowns with the ends of her blue bow "bosky acres" and "unshrubbed down"—and asks why Juno now calls her to this place. The flowers, the woods, the plains are, in Ceres' own words, her own: Ceres is Lady of the Earth, which she proclaims to be hers and the pride of which she celebrates. Iris is her crown; her function within the order of nature is that of carrying dew, but, most of all, she gifts beauty. Her portrait juxtaposes to the classical allusion no less than three extraordinary metaphorical excesses. The saffron wings come from the *Aeneid* (4.700–701), but Shakespeare ornaments Virgil's "dewy" (*roscida*) with drops of honey and refreshing showers. He then transforms the "thousand shifting tints" that the Virgilian Iris carries into the sky from the sun into a blue reflection that frames the whole world, and finally, not yet satisfied, he concludes with the image of the scarf.

All this is no more than a mere appellation ("Who, with thy saffron wings"), and Ceres' question receives a terse but crucial reply: "A contract of true love to celebrate, / And some donation freely to estate / On the blest lovers." The masque, therefore, is for Miranda and Ferdinand the theatrical sealing of their union. Venus and Cupid, Iris assures us, are absent. What Ferdinand had earlier called "lust"—the carnal union explicitly prohibited by Prospero before the wedding—is not present in the contract of love. There are instead blessings and wishes for prosperity and for offspring and descendants. This is declared in song by Juno, who invokes honor, riches, "marriage-blessing," "long continuance and increasing," and continuous joy; and Ceres is in full accord, extending the blessing to the whole earth, outlining a new Golden Age and Garden of Eden:

> Earth's increase, foison plenty,
> Barns and garners never empty;
> Vines with clust'ring bunches growing;
> Plants with goodly burthen bowing;
> Spring come to you at the farthest
> In the very end of harvest!
> Scarcity and want shall shun you;
> Ceres' blessing so is on you.
>   (4.1.110–17)

This, then, is what the union of Ferdinand and Miranda signifies: not only the love between them (and, of course, the alliance between Naples and Milan) but also its fulfillment at the beginning of a new era, in which there will be a year with no winter, and which will see their stock and the earth itself grow and be filled, according to the words of Genesis: "Be fruitful and multiply, and fill the earth."[4] Fulfillment now means "plenty," plenitude.

No wonder that Ferdinand, at this point, should exclaim: "This is a most majestic vision, and / harmonious charmingly," and that, as soon as Prospero has confirmed that he has invoked these spirits with his art to stage his own fantasies, he should add: "Let me live here ever: / So rare a wonder'd father and a wife / Makes this place a Paradise" (4.1.122–24).[5] Ferdinand recognizes once and for all that this is the Garden of Eden, which has its Eve and its Father. But the spectacle is not over yet. While Juno and Ceres whisper to each other, Iris calls in the Naiads and some harvesters, so that they may dance together, thus completing the contract of love and the ritual wish for fertility. Prospero, however, seems perturbed; he "starts suddenly" and begins to talk, while the harmonious music ends in "a strange, hollow, and confused noise" and the masque disappears, albeit "heavily," in a chaos of notes. Ferdinand and Miranda immediately observe the passion and anger that dominate the face of the Father. He remembers Caliban's and his accomplices' conspiracy, which he had forgotten and which is coming to a head, and curtly dismisses the spirits.

This is a critical moment in *The Tempest*, in which the real—the unexpected—erupts into the ideal, shattering its harmony and loading Prospero's forgetfulness with every kind of psychological implication and perhaps, most of all, with his sudden awareness of having repressed reality. Shakespeare, as ever, offers no explanation. Instead, he makes Prospero shift his uneasiness onto Ferdinand, to whom he turns and says, "You do look, my son, in a moved sort, / as if you were dismayed." But there must be something else feeding the magician's passion, for in his next words a veil of sadness and of pessimism seems to prevail. This is confirmed, in the end, when he newly declares himself perturbed, weak, and infirm, with an old, troubled brain and a beating mind, aware perhaps for the first time of his own frailness, of age, and of death. Prospero begins with the now ended spectacle and with the actors, who, he says, "were all spirits" who have melted into thin air. Then, however, he moves from the disappearance of the masque, of the theatrical illusion that he himself has organized, to a vision in which he contemplates the dissolution of the whole world: the end of human constructs, of the earth itself, and of the individual human being. It is his Apocalypse:

> You do look, my son, in a mov'd sort,
> As if you were dismay'd: be cheerful, sir.
> Our revels now are ended. These our actors,
> As I foretold you, were all spirits, and
> Are melted into air, into thin air:
> And, like the baseless fabric of this vision,
> The cloud-capp'd towers, the gorgeous palaces,
> The solemn temples, the great globe itself,
> Yea, all which it inherit, shall dissolve,
> And, like this insubstantial pageant faded,

Leave not a track behind. We are such stuff
As dreams are made on: and our little life
Is rounded with a sleep. Sir, I am vex'd;
Bear with my weakness; my old brain is troubled:
Be not disturb'd with my infirmity:
If you be pleas'd, retire into my cell,
And there repose: a turn or two I'll walk,
To still my beating mind.

(4.1.146–63)

It may be that Prospero—before the flourishing of Nature evoked by Iris and Ceres for the good of the couple who will survive him—suddenly feels the vain corruptibility of art and of life, which for him are one. He certainly inextricably ties the theatre, of which he is a master and director, and to which Jaques had already compared the world and human life in *As You Like It* (2.7.140–67), to the image of existence as a vanishing dream, which literature has known since Job (20:6–8).[6] "All the world's a stage," Jaques had proclaimed. Men and women are merely the players who interpret different parts in the seven acts that represent the seven ages of man until the end of the drama, the "Last scene of all, / that ends this strange, eventful history": a "second childishness and mere oblivion, / sans teeth, sans eyes, sans taste, sans everything." "They will fly away like a dream," Zophar had said of the wicked in the Book of Job, "and not be found; they will be chased away like a vision of the night." But in Prospero's words the sense of dissolution is insisted upon, absolute, final: the spirits have melted into the elements, into air (and Prospero adds, with another excess, "into thin air"), as if they had never existed; the fabric of the vision was "baseless" from the start, and now the scene, already without substance, is made pale and vanishes. The world will dissolve; human life is a dream crowned by sleep, and we all know that that sleep, as Hamlet said, is death. Rising in Prospero's mind is the shadow of Nothingness.

The performance is not over, however, and Prospero cannot yet say, "consummatum est." He still has to undo Caliban's and the two mariners'—the people's—band, and to stand up to the courtiers whom he has caused to shipwreck on the island. Ariel has already drawn the

drunk Trinculo, Stephano, and Caliban to the "filthy-mantled pool" behind the cell. Prospero thus prepares another spectacle to prevent the
coup and his own assassination. While he declares Caliban a devil in
whose nature education and culture could never grow (4.1.188–89),[7] he
has Ariel unfold and hang on a rope the glistening theatrical costumes
that he has worn many a time. The dazzled Stephano and Trinculo
fight over them, while Caliban urges them to think of the murder and
to leave aside those worthless rags. At this point, the noise of hunters is
heard, and "divers spirits" appear "in the shape of dogs and hounds,"
which, incited by Prospero and Ariel, pursue the three and drive them
away. This scene—from the filth- and stench-filled pool where the
three unlucky ones lose their bottles of wine, to the cries with which
Prospero and Ariel spur on the dogs, "Hey, Mountain, hey! Silver!
There it goes, Silver! Fury, Fury! There, Tyrant, there! Hark, hark!"—is
a comic one, like the one in which the devils of Dante's *Inferno* fish out
with hooks the barrators (those who sell public or church offices) immersed in boiling pitch (*Inf.* 21–22). But the punishment that Prospero
inflicts on the three conspirators is without pity, like the one inflicted
by Dante's devils on the sinners. "Go, charge my goblins," he instructs
Ariel, "that they grind their joints / With dry convulsions, shorten up
sinews / With agèd cramps, and more pinch-spotted make them / Than
pard or cat o'mountain." All his enemies are at Prospero's mercy now.
Only the final revelations remain.

FOR THESE, Shakespeare prepares a stupefying, single scene that oc-
cupies all of the fifth act. It is made of curtains that open one after the
other and depends, as already Marina's and Hermione's had done, on
delay and the suspense born from delay. The movement from one phase
of the scene to the next is now, and until virtually the last lines of the
play, the only observable movement on the stage, which is otherwise
dominated by total stillness. Contrary to what one would expect after
the apocalyptic words of the fourth act, Prospero is sure, now, of the
infallibility of his spells and of time's running towards the predeter-
mined goal. Alonso, Antonio, Sebastian, and Gonzalo are confined to
the lime grove that protects the cell from bad weather. They are prey to
folly and fear and unable to move. So much so, Ariel says, that if one

were to see them, one's "affections / would become tender." Prospero, taken aback, asks: "Dost thou think so, spirit?" And at Ariel's reply— "Mine would, sir, were I human"—Prospero makes himself human, opening himself up to compassion and forgiveness. How could he, who is of the same species and who suffers the same passions, not be moved more than a spirit, who is only air? Trained by his servant (this is a moving touch of genius on Shakespeare's part), Prospero elects reason and measure over fury, "virtue" over "vengeance." "They being penitent," he declares, "The sole drift of my purpose doth extend / Not a frown further." He then sends Ariel to fetch the prisoners.

Now alone on stage, the master renounces his art once and for all. Addressing first the elves of the hills, the brooks, the woods, and the lakes, Prospero speaks like Ovid's Medea (*Metamorphoses* 7.198–209). But he immediately begins to ornament wonderfully the ancient words, invoking Neptune, the sea ebbing on the shore, the moonlight, the midnight mushrooms. Little by little his calm voice rises from a murmured invocation to a proud, confident assertion of his own powers. He then abjures these powers, after a final request for some "heavenly music" to cast a spell on the senses of the prisoners and with the promise to break and bury his wand and to drown his book of spells for ever:

> Ye elves of hills, brooks, standing lakes and groves;
> And ye that on the sands with printless foot
> Do chase the ebbing Neptune and do fly him
> When he comes back; you demi-puppets that
> By moonshine do the green sour ringlets make,
> Whereof the ewe not bites; and whose pastime
> Is to make midnight mushrooms, that rejoice
> To hear the solemn curfew; by whose aid—
> Weak masters though ye be—I have bedimm'd
> The noontide sun, call'd forth the mutinous winds,
> And 'twixt the green sea and the azur'd vault
> Set roaring war: to the dread rattling thunder
> Have I given fire and rifted Jove's stout oak
> With his own bolt; the strong bas'd promontory
> Have I made shake and by the spurs pluck'd up

The pine and cedar: graves at my command
Have wak'd their sleepers, op'd and let 'em forth
By my so potent Art. But this rough magic
I here abjure, and, when I have required
Some heavenly music,—which even now I do,—
To work mine end upon their senses, that
This airy charm is for, I'll break my staff,
Bury it certain fathoms in the earth,
And deeper than did ever plummet sound
I'll drown my book.

(5.1.33–57)

Prospero is lord of white magic, while Medea is supreme controller of black magic. The Renaissance Milanese thus appears more delicate than the ancient, terrible woman of Colchis. At the same time, as if he were a benign Faust, Prospero possesses greater power. He addresses the elves, the minuscule spirits ("demi-puppets") who populate nature and who carry out their rites without leaving a trace: chasing the flux and reflux of the waves on the sand, outlining enchanted grass rings in the moonlight, creating nocturnal mushrooms. (Medea, on the other hand, invokes Night, the stars, Hecate, and Earth.) It is they whom Prospero has been using, whom he calls "weak masters." From the immense breadth of Nature on which the first line extends itself, Prospero chooses enchantment and mystery, airborne lightness, playfulness. On the other hand, his art is that of a god, able to cause and govern the grandest phenomena of Nature: of unleashing tempests (as indeed has happened at the beginning of the play), giving fire to thunder, shaking the land itself with earthquakes. In fact, Prospero is both Neptune and Jupiter: he gathers winds, provokes war between sea and sky, rifts oaks with the bolt of the father of the gods. Perhaps he is also something more, a shadow of the biblical Yahweh, "who stirs up the sea so that its waves roar," makes the sun set at noon and obscures the earth in daytime, opens sepulchers and resurrects the entombed.[8] The language of the Bible prevails, in these images, over that of Ovid; before Medea's formulas, the chariot of the sun simply "pales," and the ancient magician does indeed "bid . . . the ghosts to come forth from their tombs," but she neither "wakes" them nor opens the graves (*Metamorphoses* 7.208–9, 206).⁹ Prospero's action, moreover, has only one precedent in Shakespeare's work—not in the music and the medical cure with which Cerimon, in *Pericles,* gives life back to Thaisa, but in the music and in the words with which Paulina gives life to Hermione's statue: "I'll fill your grave up."

Prospero is the God of the island. How sensational and touching, therefore, is his renunciation of the art that made him such, his choice to become a man again, to accept old age and death, to enter again into effective reality, into history! He is now only lacking the revelation and then, the last step. He has traced a magic circle on the ground. Into this circle, at the sound of solemn music, now enter Alonso, Gonzalo, Sebastian, and Antonio; within it they are immobile, enchanted, bewitched. Prospero uses harmony to cure the unsettled minds, the brains boiling within the skull. He observes the dissolution of the spell, the return of senses and awareness. He praises Gonzalo, who saved him and Miranda. He blames Alonso, Sebastian, and Antonio for their faults, and he forgives them. He notes that intelligence and reason are beginning to reawaken, but that no one recognizes him yet. He then orders Ariel to fetch his hat and rapier. He will divest himself of his magician's robes and present himself before them "As I was sometime Milan."

Ariel helps him put on the clothes of the past. We are witnessing a metamorphosis, a ritual vesting. But the spirit accompanies this action with song, one of the most ethereal and playful of *The Tempest:*

> Where the bee sucks, there suck I:
> In a cowslip's bell I lie;
> There I couch when owls do cry.
> On the bat's back I do fly
> After summer merrily.
> Merrily, merrily shall I live now
> Under the blossom that hangs on the bough.
>   (5.1.88–94)

Ariel celebrates the freedom that will shortly be given back to him with a joy of life and a happiness (again highlighted by Robert Johnson's music) that transcend the last scene of *The Tempest* and project themselves on the future sky of the island, when it will be empty of strangers, of "civilized" men. Prospero understands; he calls Ariel "dainty," adding, "I shall miss thee, / But yet thou shalt have freedom." While the master, choosing to become a man, decides to return to civilization, Ariel will return to his element, air. He will not dissolve, as Prospero had predicted of the spirits, into air, but he will *be* air. He will vault in it in search of the time of abundance, Summer; he will sleep and fly with owls and bats, in the night; he will rest in a cowslip's bell, comfortable in beauty; he will live twixt flowers and branches, suspended in the plenitude of day. And he will suck flowers as the bee does, not only resting on them as the souls of Virgil's Elysium, who "stream round lustrous lilies" (*Aeneid* 6.707–9),[10] but drinking their nectar, as, by ancient tradition, poets do.

PROSPERO IMMEDIATELY sends Ariel to fetch the master and the boatswain of the Neapolitan ship. Meanwhile, the prisoners, free by now, have come to their senses. Gonzalo, still somewhat dazed, proclaims the island a place of torment, trouble, wonder, and amazement, a "fearful country." And Prospero reveals himself. In the absence of *dei ex machina*, he himself is *deus machinae*, the supreme demiurge who, having abjured his creator art, manifests himself as a human being: "*Behold*, sir king, / The wronged Duke of Milan, Prospero. / For more assurance that a living Prince / Does now speak to thee, I embrace thy body" (5.1.106–9, emphasis mine). Prospero speaks as Jesus does to his gathered disciples after the Passion: "Touch me and see; for a ghost does not have flesh and bones." And shortly afterwards, before the incredulity of those present, he repeats the Old and New Testament formula for divine identification: "know for certain / That *I am* Prospero, and that very duke / Which was thrust forth of Milan; who most strangely / Upon this shore, where you were wrack'd, was landed, / To be *lord* on't" (5.1.158–62, emphasis mine).

The strangers are full of doubts and want explanations that connect to the senses and reason (like Pericles, Cymbeline, and Polixenes); they think that this could be a bewitched vision, and yet they observe that Prospero's pulse "Beats as of flesh and blood." As their host says, the illusions of the island, which they are still experiencing, do not allow them to "Believe things certain," and "these lords / At this encounter do so much admire / That they devour their reason, and scarce think / Their eyes do offices of truth." Meanwhile, however, Alonso asks for forgiveness (shortly, echoing Lear, he will implore the forgiveness of his son), while Prospero expresses his warm gratitude to Gonzalo by embracing him. He then forgives his brother Antonio without the latter's uttering any word of repentance; but a brother has to be forgiven unconditionally—"Not seven times, but, I tell you, seventy-seven times" (Matt. 18:22). Alonso then mentions the loss of his son, which is irreparable, he says, such that "patience" cannot comfort him. Prospero replies, you have not looked for it; to me, for the same loss, patience has given the consolation of her "soft grace," so that I now accept the loss. When Alonso asks him, "You the like loss?" Prospero replies, "for I / Have lost my daughter." The two fathers now are very close; they have both lost their children, and in the same tempest. Prospero invites Alonso into his cell, which is his court. Alonso has given his dukedom back to him, and he will now reciprocate with "as good a thing," a wonder that will make him happy.

The last epiphany takes place now. In such a humble abode we do not find a Virgin and Child, but rather a young man and a young woman in love, playing chess, with her accusing him of cheating. What a peculiar invention, Adam and Eve at the chessboard: the intellectual, political, and erotic pastime of aristocratic courts. This means that from the state of pristine innocence in which Ferdinand and Miranda found themselves, they have entered (or reentered) civilization, which entails the playing of this game with its precise rules (and breaking them); it means that they share a social intimacy (since chess is reserved for the aristocracy) and a mental intimacy apparently already tested and proved. After the masque of Iris, Ceres, and Juno, which made Nature the fulfillment of their union, here is culture.

The sight of Ferdinand and Miranda playing chess must be more than a little surprising for those who believed the former to be dead and for whom the latter is a stranger, and it is a phenomenal *coup de théâtre* even for the spectator, who expects everything but a chessboard on a remote island. Alonso justifiably calls this sight a vision and mirage and

blesses the son he has found again. But Shakespeare lingers only a moment on the astonishment of the newcomers. Instead, he focuses on one
who is looking out from the scene itself—on Miranda, who grew up in
isolation, far from human community. The sudden appearance of so
many human beings is for her a true wonder, the revelation of a beauty
and newness never before contemplated:

> O, wonder!
> How many goodly creatures are there here!
> How beauteous mankind is! O brave new world,
> That has such people in 't!
>
> (5.1.181–84)

It is, of course, paradoxical that Miranda, who has so far lived on an
island that is like a shadow of the New World, should consider as new
a world made up of human beings coming from the Old World. It is
doubly paradoxical that she should think of a world represented by beings just like her as new, as Prospero appropriately observes: "'Tis new
to thee." But it is the beauty of humanity that gives her the impression
of newness: "O brave new world, / That has such people in 't!" In other
words, it is discovery—and precisely discovering beings just like her—
that unlocks for her a new world. With her innocence, which makes her
multiply by six Ferdinand's initial epiphany, Miranda replies to the melancholy of Hamlet, who had considered the "goodly frame" of the earth
a "sterile promontory," and man, "the beauty of the world," a "quintessence of dust." She reminds us that keeping intact our recognition of
human splendor, our astonishment at discovering what is old as if it
were new, is necessary for hope. Underlying Miranda's exclamations
we find the expectation that humanity has always nurtured for a new
heaven and a new earth, the expectation expressed by Isaiah and echoed
by Peter: "For I am about to create new heavens and a new earth; the
former things shall not be remembered or come to mind. But be glad
and rejoice for ever in what I am creating" (Isa. 65:17–18; 2 Pet. 3:13).
But Miranda now sees the new world almost as if she were in the posi-
tion of the protagonist of Revelation: "Then I saw a new heaven and a
new earth" (21:1). For her, the expectation has been fulfilled.

In its last lines *The Tempest* returns to its initial scenes, as if to close a circle, and comes ever closer to the sacred. When Alonso asks his son about the young woman with whom he was playing chess, he adds, just as Ferdinand had observed in meeting Miranda, "Is she [a] goddess?" (5.1.187; 1.2.422). When Ferdinand replies, "Sir, she is mortal / but by immortal providence she's mine," he echoes Prospero's words in response to Miranda's inquiry at the beginning of the play (5.1.189; 1.2.159). The recognition of providential action, so surprising at the end of *Hamlet*, here envelops *The Tempest*, which otherwise is dominated by Fortune and by the rigid directions of Prospero. It is Gonzalo who expresses this in the most complete manner, invoking divine blessing on the young couple:

> I have inly wept,
> Or should have spoke ere this. Look down, you gods,
> And on this couple drop a blessèd crown,
> For it is you that have chalked forth the way
> Which brought us hither.
>
>   (5.1.200–204)

Alonso then pronounces the first *amen* of this ending: "I say amen, Gonzalo." At this point Gonzalo summarizes the action of *The Tempest*, interpreting it from a providential perspective. The Duke of Milan was expelled from Milan so that his descendants could become kings of Naples; in a single voyage, Claribel found a husband in Tunis and her brother Ferdinand a wife "where he himself was lost"; Prospero found his dukedom in a "poor isle," "and all of us ourselves, / When no man was his own." Gonzalo seems not to account for the lack of repentance on the part of Antonio and Sebastian, but his rediscovery of himself, the regeneration and birth of the "new man" in himself and in Alonso, are indicated with great clarity. When, immediately afterwards, Alonso invites Ferdinand and Miranda to give him their hands and pronounces the solemn warning—"Let grace and sorrow still embrace his heart / that doth not wish you joy"—Gonzalo replies with a double *amen:* "Be it so! Amen."

There remain, in the simple, intricate plot of *The Tempest*, two knots to untangle: the destiny of the Neapolitan crew, and that of the three conspirators, Stephano, Trinculo, and Caliban. In quick succession, Ariel leads them all to the cell. He awakens the crew, asleep under the hatches, by means of strange noises, roaring, shrieking, howling, and jingling chains, and returns the ship to a pristine condition ("These are not natural events," comments Alonso, "they strengthen from strange to stranger"). He transports the men "On a trice . . . / Even in a dream" before the others (Alonso insists: "This is as strange a maze as e'er men trod, / And there is in this business more than nature / Was ever conduct of"). Then, he frees Caliban and the other two conspirators and drives them towards the cell. The scene becomes comic— Stephano and Trinculo still being drunk—but with an underlying, striking seriousness. Indeed, arriving before his master, Caliban invokes his god, Setebos, and is astonished at the sight of the beauty of the courtiers and of Prospero (this is Miranda's own reaction transferred to the "savage"): "O Setebos, these be brave spirits indeed! / How fine my master is! I am afraid / He will chastise me." But Prospero does not punish him; he calls him "misshapen knave" and "demi-devil," recalls his being born of a witch and a devil, but acknowledges him as his own. He then sends Caliban into the cell together with the other two, to restore order in it, "As," he says, "you look / to have my pardon." And Caliban repents, acknowledges having been a "thrice-double ass" to take Stephano for a god, and promises from now on to "be wise" and to "seek for grace."

Prospero does not punish Caliban; rather, he foreshadows his forgiveness of him, allowing him once again to enter the cell from which he had banned him. More importantly, he makes Caliban his own: "This thing of darkness," he proclaims before everyone, "I acknowledge mine." The colonizer takes responsibility for the colonized. The magician who has renounced his art, the God who has made himself man again, adopts Caliban, becomes father of the "other," of darkness, of the being "as disproportioned in his manners / as in his shape," whom he considers a son of the devil, who has conspired against his life and attempted to rape his daughter. Perhaps Prospero's new behavior is not disconnected from the recognition that darkness was present also in his own spirit, in his practicing magic, in his conquering and enslaving the native Caliban. But in his present gesture there is a moral grandness out of the ordinary, an assuming of responsibility and paternity that transcends human ethics, as if it were that of a Christ who takes upon himself the sin of the world.

It is thus not a coincidence that, after promising to tell his story, preparing his return to Italy, stating that upon arriving back in Milan "every third thought shall be [his] grave," and saying goodbye to his "chick" Ariel, Prospero should appear on stage, alone, to recite the Epilogue, in which he declares himself to be by now devoid of spells, of strength, of spirits, and of art, and to be fully in the hands of the members of the audience. From these, following theatrical conventions for Epilogues, he asks for prayer, concluding with two lines in which the presence of the Christian Gospel is extremely clear:

> Now I want
> Spirits to enforce, art to enchant,
> And my ending is despair
> Unless I be relieved by prayer,
> Which pierces so that it assaults
> Mercy itself and frees all faults.
> As you from crime would pardon'd be,
> Let your indulgence set me free.[11]
> (Epilogue, 13–20)

The echo resounding in Prospero's last words is no less than that of the Lord's Prayer: first, "deliver us from evil," and then the invitation with which Jesus seals the prayer he has just taught his disciples. "For if you forgive others their trespasses, your heavenly Father will also forgive you; but if you do not forgive others, neither will your Father forgive your trespasses" (Matt. 6:14–15).

LET ME SUMMARIZE. *The Tempest* possesses many facets and many meanings. It is set in an enchanted island and in a maze that should lie somewhere between Tunis and Naples, but which is clearly also in the shadow of Africa and of the New World, and also of the Earthly Paradise, the kingdom of heaven on earth. The play contains a multiplicity of discourses and presents one problem after another, or rather one problem within another: discourses on power, utopia, colonialism and "savages," family relationships, eros, nature and culture, folly and reason, conscience, knowledge, language, and magic and sorcery. It often does so obliquely; for example, it is clear that the family relationships of significance are, in the first instance, those between father and daughter and between father and son. But, it has been noted, the former seems colored by jealousy and perhaps tainted by incest, and there is no mention of Prospero's and Alonso's wives. The world of *The Tempest*, unlike that of the other romances, and with the crucial exception of Miranda, is exclusively male. In the same way, eros is clearly concentrated in the relationship between Miranda and Ferdinand, a love at first sight that, however, needs to remain chaste until marriage. But one also cannot forget that Miranda, the only woman of the island and of the play, is the inevitable object of the violent desire of Caliban, who tried to rape her and who offers her to Stephano as reward for the elimination of Prospero.

In similar fashion, the discourse on power seems, at the very least, double-faceted. Prospero is an enlightened lord but also a tyrant; he lost the dukedom of Milan because of his brother's coup, but also because he neglected government in favor of his studies. Furthermore, Gonzalo's utopia is beautiful but is in no way realizable; Stephano's and Trinculo's colonization is subjected to mockery, but Prospero's is at once exalted and contested; Caliban is a monstrous savage but with feelings at once violent and delicate, and he rightly wants his freedom. The very succession of residence and domination looks like that of English history, which Shakespeare knew so well: a series of foreign usurpations (Romans and then Anglo-Saxons on Celtic Britons, Normans on Anglo-Saxons) by which Ariel, the original native, innocent and free, is imprisoned and supplanted by Sycorax and Caliban, and the latter is subjected by Prospero.

Nature is never seen, but it is sung by Ariel and projected by the Edenic, pastoral masque; culture is a supreme value, but we are shown its excesses, both in Prospero's tyranny and in the conspiracy of Antonio and Sebastian, seemingly civilized men, against Alonso. Language, which is the manifestation of culture, and which is necessary to establish the love between Ferdinand and Miranda, is used by Caliban only to curse. Reason is celebrated as being superior to folly, but it reveals itself as completely useless for comprehending the island's mysteries. Prospero's magic has positive value but appears to trespass into Medea's sorcery. His knowledge and wisdom are divine, but after the masque that he ordered Ariel to stage, he is perturbed and contemplates in desolation the dissolution of the illusions that he created and of the whole world. For every good there is an evil, as always on earth.

But also, for every evil there is a good. What seems to me to reign supreme is wonder—it frames *The Tempest,* penetrates into its joints, imbues its characters, and even gives its name to its only woman, Miranda. It sometimes transforms itself into terror, but it remains nonetheless an astonishment that predisposes one's spirit to the desire for knowledge, to the encounter with the other, to love, and to the acceptance of the unexpected and of mystery. Wonder, so Plato and Aristotle said, generates the love of wisdom: philosophy and inquiry into the phenomena of nature. Aristotle takes a further step: wonder, according to him, is also at the origin of poetry, because myth, he argues, concerns wonderful things.[12] In the romances, Shakespeare is the *poietés* who is enchanted before the mystery of things, which he takes upon himself as Lear would like to do. And he transfers such astonishment onto his characters, his scenes, and his audience.

There is an evil and a good for all things, from the expulsion of Prospero and Miranda from Milan and their arrival on the island to the final resolution of the plot, which, however, does not entail the conversion and repentance of Sebastian and of Antonio. The discussion on good and evil continues, as we have seen, until the last lines of the Epilogue. But wonder has the power to present the good as the beautiful in the *kalokagathia,* which *The Tempest* shares with the other romances and which it celebrates with even greater intensity. Beauty is suffused through each of the crucial scenes, right from the words with which Ariel recalls the "deep nook" where he was once invoked at midnight to procure for Prospero the dew of the Bermudas. It is into the beauty of coral and pearls that Alonso is transmuted. Beautiful, indeed extremely beautiful does Ferdinand appear to Miranda. Beautiful, lush, and green is the grass of the island for Gonzalo. Beautiful is the union of the two young people, according to Prospero. Beautiful is the vision of the clouds that Caliban sees opening up to reveal unheard-of riches. Iris gifts the beauty of dew. And the world is colored by infinite *pulchritudo* in the masque and in Prospero's farewell to his art. Beautiful does Prospero appear to Caliban in the last scene. And finally, beauty shines in the creatures whom Miranda contemplates while playing chess with Ferdinand: beautiful is humanity, beautiful is the world.

Where beauty reaches, there lie redemption and salvation. When the music that resounds throughout *The Tempest* tunes its notes, then are astonishment and enchantment born. When music is broken into disharmony—as at the end of the masque—chaos and despair enter into the world and the spirit. Music is the objective correlative of art; the most ethereal of the arts, it is entrusted to Ariel, who transforms it into sublime poetry. It is earthly and heavenly, and the echo on the island of the harmony of the spheres. It perturbs, wounds, heals, and saves. From "Come unto these yellow sands" to "Where the bee sucks, there suck I," music calls forth yearning, nostalgia, the desire for freedom; it calls forth beauty and goodness that long for plenitude.

True, Art can trespass into sorcery, it produces nothing but illusions that will dissolve in air, and it knows how to upset the world. However, as in *The Winter's Tale,* it is also able to resurrect the dead; it molds events, gives them direction, stirs up repentance, and spurs conversion. Art, a kind of ancestor of our omnipotent modern technology, is dangerous and salvific at the same time. It is the art not only of Giulio Romano but also that of Faust. Unlike Faust, however, Prospero renounces it, abjures it, and divests himself of its garments. (Is this also an admonition for us, who are infatuated with our technology?)

As the demonstration—as true exhibit, unfolding, divine manifestation—of the art of William Shakespeare, there are in *The Tempest* both the spirits of goodness and the sons of evil, both Ariel and Caliban, but also Gonzalo, Antonio, and Sebastian. All the elements are present: Ariel's air, fire, and water, Caliban's earth, the sea that surrounds the island, and its sky. There is the weightiness, slowness, and stolidity of Caliban, the cannibal, the savage, the deformed slave, the devil, but also the legitimate owner of the island, possessing an acute sensitivity. On the other hand, vaulting in the air is the lightness, quickness, and intelligence of Ariel, his ability to transform himself and to suggest, his readiness at his master's call ("here I am," he says, like the Abraham of the Bible: *hinne-ni*), but also his desire for freedom and his ability to contest, love, and forgive. Ariel, an elf, is a ubiquitous and faithful angel; a minister of music and dance, sublime nature, potential poet; a "Lion of God" able to flame on the endangered ship, but also an "altar" of the Lord.[13]

It is difficult to imagine that a design as vast as that of *The Tempest* should not also contain a theological discourse, that is, a consideration of the role played by the divine in the cosmos and in individual destinies. It is interesting, for example, that the providence invoked at the beginning by Prospero is replaced shortly after by Fortune, which he believes to be his "lady." Combined with his "prescience" (1.2.180), however, chance is first transformed, in the words of the harpy Ariel to the courtiers, into destiny, "that hath to instrument this lower world," then into fate and into implacable retributive justice, and then again, in Ferdinand's words to his father, into "immortal providence" (3.3.53; 5.1.189). To each according to his ability to discern and according to the degree of his conversion; to distinguish providence from chance and from necessity one needs inward and outward openness. Possessing both, in the end, are Ferdinand and Gonzalo, who recognize that it is the gods who have traced the route that brought the two courts onto the island. Not possessing either, however, are Alonso, Antonio, and Sebastian when Ariel appears before them as a harpy to stage the phantom banquet; against them, then, who are pagan in their inner being, is the threat of fate's punishment.

Let us also consider history: it is recalled in connection with *before* (by Prospero and Miranda), and a return to it is imagined for *after*, with the voyage back to Naples and Milan. During the action, history appears to be suspended. Prospero and Miranda live *outside* it, but history bursts into their Eden with the tempest and the arrival of the Neapolitans on the island. On one level, the two parallel projects for a coup—by Antonio and Sebastian, on the one hand, and by Caliban and his accomplices, on the other—constitute the attempt to bring effective history onto the island. With the elimination of Prospero and Alonso, Naples would not change, but the island would become like Naples,

Milan, or an English colony in America. Prospero makes sure that such an attempt fails, that history resumes its course only after having been purified, straightened, and corrected. His action, like God's and Joseph's in Genesis, is aimed at turning evil into good, at ensuring, that is, that the story of salvation has an effect on earthly history. In the second scene of the play, Prospero invites Miranda to listen for a little longer to the story of their expulsion from Milan and of their arrival onto the island: "I'll bring thee," he says, "to the present business / which now's upon 's, *without the which, this story / were most impertinent*" (1.2.136–38, emphasis mine). Prospero is talking not only of his story but also of the history to which it refers: the action that is upon them, its intervention, will change history, will give it purpose, an end. It will transform it from a succession of casual events or of events willed by others into a teleological sequence.

Let us think, finally, about the intertextual texture of *The Tempest*. Placed at crucial junctures of the play are citations, reminiscences, allusions to Virgil and Ovid, to Montaigne, and to the accounts of contemporary travelers to the New World. These confer on the action a temporal and spatial vastness that ranges from antiquity to modernity, from Carthage and Tunis to the Bermudas, and a set of profound mythical, psychological, and political resonances that in the abyss of memory reach to Dido and Medea. Moreover, there appear in *The Tempest* countless "shapes": harpies, pagan deities, elves, nymphs. There is a native god, or at least a god whose cult was established before the arrival of the Christians: Setebos, the god of Sycorax and of her son Caliban (and in truth a god of Patagonia). At a certain point, idolatry manifests itself: through Caliban, who, like the native of the Americas meeting the European, adores as a god the stranger who offers him inebriation. And, seen against the light, there is also the devil, whom Prospero refers to as Caliban's father (1.2.321–22). In short, *The Tempest* unfolds a pantheon of gods next to whom, as sometimes happens to the Yahweh of the Old Testament, the God of the Christians appears powerless or on the verge of disappearing.

We should not forget all this. But we should also remember that *The Tempest* (almost) opens with the Creation of Genesis, when Caliban remembers that, as soon as Prospero arrived on the island, he taught him "how / To name the bigger light, and how the less, / That burn by day and night" (1.2.335–36; Gen. 1:16). And it (almost) ends with a vision worthy of Revelation, when Prospero reveals to the astonished Ferdinand that the spectacle is over and that now "The cloud-capp'd towers, the gorgeous palaces, / The solemn temples, the great globe itself, / Yea, all which it inherit, shall dissolve" (4.1.152–54). One could even argue that *The Tempest* begins with a boiling abyss—the chaos of the Beginning, which opens the Bible, like the tempest that opens the play—and ends with the "new earth," which, prophesied by Isaiah, is seen in Revelation; when Miranda, surprised at the appearance of so many human beings, exclaims: "O brave new world."[14]

Embedded within the core of *The Tempest* is a plot whose action bears all the characteristics of the sacred. It opens with the Edenic scene in which Ferdinand and Miranda play the role of Adam and Eve, who meet for the first time and fall in love. This scene continues in the second encounter between the two and will have a further, ideal continuation in the message of growth and multiplication invoked by the masque of Iris, Ceres, and Juno, while just before this a banquet placed somewhere between Virgil and Isaiah is denied to the sinners. The crucial epiphanies of *The Tempest* concern this Man and this Woman in the Garden of Eden. Of such an Earthly Paradise Prospero is God (implicitly contrasted with Setebos), able to stir up tempests, to direct the action, and to reveal himself. But Prospero, who is master, supreme magician, poet, director, and actor of *The Tempest,* decides to become human once again. He makes a choice similar to Christ's: he divests himself and takes on the likeness of human beings (Phil. 2:7). A divinity who had exited from history, he now reenters it; he is a *numen* of wisdom and art who can commit errors, like a human being, and who will shortly dedicate one thought out of three to his grave; a god of flesh, immanent, perishable, human.

This god examines himself, is perturbed, shows himself full of passion and anger, and knows the agony of him who foreshadows the end, Christ in Gethsemane. He is led to mercy by his servant Ariel, as, on the road to Sodom, God is led to justice by Abraham. He then forgives (he even forgives those who do not repent, who know not what they are doing), and issues an invitation to patience and repentance. He makes those who were lost find themselves again, drives those who are willing to accept his invitation to reach towards their true selves. He takes sins upon himself. He thus initiates a conversion in which repentance and the recognition of providence dominate. Evil does not entirely disappear; Antonio and Sebastian do not repent. But good prevails, and the blessings, the *amen* of the final scene, would seal *The Tempest* in glory and joy even if there did not appear in the very last lines the evangelical invocation of our forgiving others their trespasses, just as we wish our trespasses to be forgiven.

The Good News of *The Tempest* is all here, in these *amen*s and in humility invoking forgiveness of sins. And this is Shakespeare's testament: a human and divine New Testament of wonder and beauty, of meditation and endurance, of death and suffering, of life and joy. The invention of this Gospel—its composition in parables, images, "shapes," illusions, words—is one of the greatest legacies that the magician, demiurge, poet, creator William Shakespeare has bequeathed to us.

Conclusion

How beautiful upon the mountains are the feet of him that bringeth good

tidings, that publisheth peace; that bringeth good tidings of good, that

publisheth salvation; that saith unto Zion, Thy God reigneth!

I do not know whether Shakespeare believed, in his most intimate self, in the immortality of the soul or in the resurrection of the flesh. He does, however, make flesh resurrect here, now, before our very eyes, in Thaisa and Hermione. And, I think, if we were able to believe in this supreme fiction of his, it would be enough to draw us closer to Paul's words in the First Letter to the Corinthians (15:12–13): "Now if Christ be preached that he rose from the dead, how say some among you that there is no resurrection of the dead? But if there be no resurrection of the dead, then is Christ not risen: and if Christ be not risen, then is our preaching vain, and your faith is also vain." If—suspending disbelief, as we are invited to do by Samuel Coleridge—we are able to believe, in interacting with a work of art, that a sculpture is a person (Hermione), then we do not have far to go to take the leap of faith (requested by Paulina) to believe in resurrection.

The happiness brought to us by the Good News of Shakespeare's romances has the splendor of the glory and the humility of small things, and it is always at risk of vanishing. The masque in *The Tempest*, with Iris, Ceres, and Juno, gives us a vision of abundance, re-creation, and Edenic multiplication; but Prospero is troubled by it and immediately pronounces an apocalyptic prophecy about the dissolution of the cosmos. The music of the spheres is heard by Pericles on recognizing Marina, by which he is enchanted and put to sleep: by comparison to the masque, this is a briefer, more subjective, and therefore perhaps more perfectly intense and unquestionable moment. And then there is the effulgent glory shining at the end of *Cymbeline* in and through the light that imbues the exchange of gazes and everything touched by it: this is perhaps a more enduring glory, because it is *human* and *reciprocal*. "See," says the king, "Posthumus anchors upon Imogen: / And she *(like harmless lightning) throws her eye* / On him: her brothers, me: her master *hitting / Each object with a joy:* the counterchange / Is severally in all" (emphasis mine).

Perhaps, for Shakespeare, the greatest glory resides in small and ephemeral things, like the flowers, for example, picked by Ophelia, Marina, Guiderius and Arviragus, and Perdita. They are flowers of the field: daffodils, "That come before the swallow dares, and take / The winds of March with beauty"; violets, "dim, / But sweeter than the lids of Juno's eyes / Or Cytherea's breath"; pale primroses; the flower-de-luce; lilies. Yes, lilies, flowers of the field; Shakespeare seems to follow with fervor the words of Jesus: "Consider the lilies, how they grow: they neither toil nor spin; yet I tell you even Solomon in all his glory was not clothed like one of these." Perhaps this is where the greatest glory resides: "in a cowslip's bell," as Ariel sings, "under the blossom that hangs on the bough."

This kind of glory is beauty, the *pulchritudo* of the world and of human beings. It is the "beauty" of the daffodils, which in their beauty are able to "take / The winds of March" (poetry constantly captures and stuns us with such marvelous, sudden, and flashing excesses; flowers bewitch the winds of March with their humble splendor). It is the beauty of Florizel according to Perdita, and that of Ferdinand and the whole of humanity in the eyes of Miranda. In the romances, such beauty often takes the form of the *kalokagathia,* the indissoluble union of the good and the beautiful, professed since the time of Plato and handed down in and through philosophy, poetry, painting, and sculpture until and throughout the Renaissance. It is the *pulchritudo* of being, the clarity, as in Perdita's case, of the *tode-ti,* of being-this-now. We are dealing here with a Greek ideal, which would at first seem to have little to do with the Old and New Testaments. Yet beauty had inserted itself in the Hebrew Bible as soon as it had been transposed into Greek; where the original Genesis proclaims that God saw that light and every other part of Creation were good (*tob*), the Septuagint has "beautiful" (*kalón*). In fact, Ecclesiastes had already confidently declared that God "made everything beautiful in its time" (3:11), and the Psalms (in the Geneva Bible) proclaim that "His worke is beautiful and glorious" (111:3). With the Bible's arrival in the West in both Greek and Latin, the beauty of the cosmos found its legitimate place also within Christianity, thus penetrating into the Middle Ages and reaching the Renaissance (when, in fact, Platonism itself was being rediscovered).

The seeds of beauty were clearly already there in the Hebrew Scriptures. The Song of Songs celebrates the Bride: "Thou art fair, my love; behold, thou art fair; thou hast doves' eyes within thy locks" (4:1). And if this justifies consideration of the beauty of the human being, one need only read Isaiah (52:7) to find the exhaltation of the Good News: "How beautiful upon the mountains are the feet of him that bringeth good tidings, that publisheth peace; that bringeth good tidings of good, that publisheth salvation; that saith unto Zion, Thy God reigneth!" The connection between *pulchritudo* and the announcement of peace, of goodness, and of salvation is crucial, and indeed Paul repeats this crucial move in his Letter to the Romans (10:15), citing Isaiah in speaking precisely of the preaching of the Good News: "And how shall they preach, except they be sent? as it is written, How beautiful are the feet of them that preach the gospel of peace, and bring glad tidings of good things!"[1]

Beauty, then, is also a fundamental part of Scripture in general and of the Gospels. What truly counts, as Harold Fisch puts it in commenting on the passage from Isaiah cited above, is not beauty, which is static, in perfect equilibrium, but rather "the message that the herald is yet to deliver and which, in fact, he will deliver only when his feet have stopped running. In the meantime, that undelivered message sheds beauty on his moving feet—the beauty of an annunciation." And further, "If we can think of this scene in Isaiah 52:7 in terms of the art of painting, then the figure of the messenger will have to be striving for something outside the painting, some yet-to-be disclosed image of glad tidings."[2] The beauty of which Fisch speaks is thus eminently dramatic, and it is particularly appropriate to link to the romances, which (with the exception of the first part of the final scene of *The Tempest*) are all characterized by whirling motion in space and time: through the whole Mediterranean and the whole of Marina's youth, in *Pericles;* between Britain and Rome, and mountains and woods, in *Cymbeline;* between Sicily and Bohemia and through the sixteen years that pass between Perdita's birth and recovery in *The Winter's Tale;* between one part of the island and another, through the maze, and in a time situated between Milan's *before* and Naples' and Milan's *after,* in *The Tempest.*[3]

The epitome of such movement is Prospero's airy minister, Ariel. Light, invisible, ubiquitous, and perennially changing in form, Ariel flies instantaneously from the ship on which he looks like a flame to the yellow sands that he evokes to Ferdinand, from "the deep nook, where once / Thou call'dst me up at midnight to fetch dew / From the still-vex'd Bermudas," to his master's cell. By contrast, the march of the Neapolitan-Milanese courtiers from the site of the shipwreck to Prospero's cell is slow, wearisome, and labyrinthine; whereas the march of Caliban and his accomplices towards the same place is disaster-prone, inebriated, and quarrelsome, and in fact only leads them to a filth- and stench-filled pool. Everything moves in Shakespeare's universe, and the thing most resembling the feet of Isaiah's and Paul's messenger are the "printless feet" with which the elves chase "ebbing Neptune" in the great speech with which Prospero abandons his magic art.

In the light of this intense and pronounced motion, moments of stasis acquire even greater relevance, as pauses suspended between time and eternity, characterized by an earthly, immanent fixity that evokes an imminent and transcendent beyond—immobile Pericles on the ship in the port of Mytilene; Posthumus anchored on Imogen, the other characters locked in a reciprocal exchange of gazes; the statue of Hermione, before which those present fall silent; the motionless, alienated folly of Alonso, Antonio, Sebastian, and Gonzalo. This is a world full of altarpieces, in which we see the astonishing effects of expectant, rapturous waiting, of immobile ecstasies, of epiphanies, of transfigurations.

Quickest, lightest, and most volatile of all, however, is the motion of music. Music is always present in Shakespearian drama and appears at all the crucial moments of the romances, not just as decoration, but also in an evocative, enchanting, celebratory, restorative role. It is with music, even before, with her extraordinary story, that Marina awakens Pericles, and the scene that opens with her song ends with the music of the spheres. (I would like to underscore once again that, according to the long tradition on which Shakespeare is here building,[4] human beings *cannot* hear such music: what happens to Pericles is a sign of transcendent illumination.) In *Cymbeline* (2.3.19–25), there sounds an *aubade* that sings of lark and dawn, and which, despite the arrogance of Cloten's intentions towards Imogen, delightfully celebrates "every thing that pretty is." Also in *Cymbeline,* we have Guiderius' and Arviragus' dirge for Fidele (Imogen), a *memento mori* and invitation to final "consummation" among the most intense ever to be composed. "Solemn music" accompanies the apparition of Posthumus' ancestors, protesting against Jupiter. In *The Winter's Tale,* Autolycus the thief sings, while Perdita both sings and dances; but the most powerful music here is that invoked by Paulina so as to give life to Hermione's statue: "Music, awake her; strike! / 'Tis time; descend; be stone no more." The union of music and sculpture signals the miraculous reunion of spirit and flesh: the most ethereal of the arts breathes life into the solid, marble image, into the most material of all the arts. We are not given to know exactly which notes are evoked by Paulina. But the instrument can only be, following Scripture, a trumpet. From Zephaniah (1:15–16) onwards (and then again in the *Dies irae*), this is always the instrument that reawakens the flesh on the Day of Judgment; and the central passage in the First Letter to the Corinthians (15:52), memorably set to music by Handel, reads: "The trumpet shall sound, and the dead shall be raised incorruptible, and we shall be changed."[5]

We thus return to *The Tempest,* which makes music its connective tissue and one of the principal sources of its enchantment. Music is ever sounding in the play: luring ("Come unto these yellow sands"), confusing ("The watch-dogs bark"), intriguing ("Full fathom five"), soporific, and awakening. It issues from mouths intoxicated by wine, yet it is at the same time a hymn to liberty and revolt. It spreads from a timbrel and a flute to the vibrations of a thousand instruments. Music in *The Tempest* is strange and solemn, in preparation for the banquet; sweet, so as to scold but also so as to open the masque; dark and confusing, so as to signal the masque's sudden end; solemn again, so as to sanction Prospero's rejection of his art and to introduce the courtiers into the final scene; light, as a foretaste of liberty ("Where the bee sucks"). In short, music in *The Tempest* is the sound track of a show that in many respects foreshadows modern cinema.

In the romances, music is not only the handmaiden of poetry but also a lady of Art and wonder. It invents themes and deepens motifs, creates illusions, regenerates, resurrects, and bewitches. Wonder is, indeed, the dominant state of being in these works. One emblematic moment is in *The Winter's Tale:* before the full Sicilian court, before Perdita, Florizel, and Polixenes, in the chapel inside the gallery of her palace, Paulina draws the curtain and reveals the statue of Hermione. "I like your silence," she says, "it the more shows off / Your wonder." The same phenomenon occurs when Prospero reveals Ferdinand and Miranda playing chess. Here, however, it is one of the characters *in* the apparent mirage who gives voice to astonishment: "O wonder!" Cymbeline calls it "rare instinct." Pericles sees it as "the rarest dream that e'er dull sleep / Did mock sad fools withal."

Wonder. Dante defines it as "dizziness of spirit" and says that it rises from seeing, hearing, and perceiving "great and marvelous things," thus urging us towards reverence, veneration, and the desire for knowledge (*Convivio* 4.25.5). Shakespeare spreads it liberally among the characters (to one of whom he gives its name, Miranda) and in the scenes of his last plays. Sometimes, he makes wonder trespass into fear, but it is always presented as the spirit's openness to encounter with the "other," to love, to acceptance of the unexpected and the mysterious. As stated earlier, according to Plato and Aristotle, wonder generates the love of wisdom—philosophy and the investigation of natural phenomena; and for Aristotle, wonder is also at the origin of poetry, because myth concerns wonderful things.

It is to wonderful things that the late Shakespeare turns his attention, an enchanted *poietés* before the mystery of things that he now takes upon himself. But only once in his works does Shakespeare speak explicitly of the activity of the poet. This occurs in *A Midsummer Night's Dream* (which clearly has a number of fantastic elements in common with the romances), when the rationalist Theseus, who tells his future wife Hippolyta that he does not believe in "antique fables" and "fairy toys," describes ironically the lunatic, the lover, and the poet. The three, he says, "Are of imagination all compact":

> One sees more devils than vast hell can hold.
> That is the madman: the lover, all as frantic,
> Sees Helen's beauty in a brow of Egypt:
> The poet's eye, in a fine frenzy rolling,
> Doth glance from heaven to earth, from earth to heaven;
> And as imagination bodies forth
> The forms of things unknown, the poet's pen
> Turns them to shapes, and gives to airy nothing
> A local habitation and a name.
> Such tricks hath strong imagination
> That if it would but apprehend some joy,
> It comprehends some bringer of that joy.
>
> (5.1.9–20)

The passage is ultimately inspired by Platonic ideas, taken up again first in the Italian and then in the English Renaissance (by Sir Philip Sidney and George Puttenham, for example). The "frenzy" of which Theseus speaks is the *furor poeticus* theorized by Democritus. Despite the irony, Shakespeare describes the effects of such *furor* with precision; as Theseus says above, the poet turns his gaze from heaven to earth and from earth to heaven and then, in the same way as the imagination creates forms of unknown things, he gives them shape. Theseus adds that when fantasy seeks joy, it has such power as to invent "the bringer" of joy. This last idea would mean that Isaiah, in exalting the beauty of good tidings, creates the messenger conveying them; whereas the previous sentences describe the work of Shakespeare the playwright in *A Midsummer Night's Dream* and the romances, which, as we have seen, constantly present us with motion from heaven to earth and vice versa, and with the making concrete of "airy nothing."

Traditionally, the inspiration provided by the poet's madness was thought to be divine in origin: its principal figures (Theseus would say "bringers") in classical and Renaissance imagination are the Muses. Even the inspiration of biblical authors comes from above, from God. It is in this way that tradition regarded Moses, as a mere scribe of the Pentateuch.[6] Prophetic and Wisdom literature (especially Job and the Psalms) are dominated by wonder (and fear) before the works of Yahweh. We could say, in summary, that the poet, enchanted by astonishment and inspired by heaven, sings wonderful and "unknown" things, uttering veiled truths.

That Shakespeare is capable of conceiving (and making fun of) himself as an inspired poet prey to *furor* appears to me certain, in virtue of the fact that the cited passage is found in *A Midsummer Night's Dream*, where, anticipating *The Tempest*, Shakespeare himself presents the fantastic story of Oberon and Titania and, within it, that of Pyramus and Thisbe. Shakespeare never assumes, as Dante does in the *Commedia*, the role of *scriba Dei*, of God's scribe, nor does he ever declare that both heaven and earth have crafted his works. He never speaks of *his* Art, *his* inspiration. I believe that he would be happy to be thought of as a spy of God, in its double meaning of someone who on God's behalf explores the human spirit and human vicissitudes, and of someone who wants to gain insight into God's own intimate being. I would, however, like to propose a further step. Wonder is not only a Greek matter, from the *Odyssey* to the late-antique romances that are the archetypes for Shakespeare's own. Wonder also pervades the Gospels, in which Jesus' birth (with the epiphany to the shepherds) and miracles (from the calming of the storm to the barren fig tree, from the empty tomb to the resurrection), generate infinite wonder in those who witness them.[7] As we have seen, the Shakespeare of the late plays speaks precisely of such phenomena. Is he not, after all, writing *his* own Gospel?

Notes

Introduction

1. After these plays, Shakespeare wrote, or at least contributed to the composition of, *Henry VIII* and *The Two Noble Kinsmen*. For an examination of the meaning of "late" and "last" in the expression "Shakespeare's late (or 'last') plays," see G. McMullan, *Shakespeare and the Idea of Late Writing: Authorship in the Proximity of Death* (Cambridge: Cambridge University Press, 2007).

2. And already from the "first" *Hamlet*, at lines 2125–2126 of the First Quarto (Q1) of 1603, where Hamlet refers to the providence in the fall of a sparrow. *Il primo Amleto*, ed. A. Serpieri (Venice: Marsilio, 1997).

Chapter 1. Amen for the Fall of a Sparrow

1. Purgatory does not exist in the Anglican afterlife, but the context of lines 1.5.9–13 is clear: the ghost says that he has been condemned to wander in the night for a certain time and to fast in fire during the day until the crimes he committed in life are "burnt and purg'd away." See also Stephen Greenblatt, *Hamlet in Purgatory* (Princeton: Princeton University Press, 2001).

2. See Harold Jenkins' commentary in *Hamlet* (Arden Shakespeare, 1982), 387.

3. Ophelia does what Hamlet only desires and pretends to do: she goes mad and (maybe) kills herself. The Ophelia who makes "fantastic garlands . . . / Of crow-flowers, nettles, daisies, and long purples" (4.7.166–67) seems the archetype of the "maiden and flowers" of the romances.

4. Jenkins underlines in his commentary that the Elizabethans believed in both a general providence, manifest in the order of creation, and, within this, a singular or special providence, manifest in particular events. Calvin insisted on the latter.

5. Luke 12:35–40 and Matthew 24:44, as suggested by Harold Fisch, *The Biblical Presence in Shakespeare, Milton, and Blake* (Oxford: Clarendon Press, 1999), 113.

6. Both the Vulgate and the King James, as well as the Geneva Bible, refer to a lonely sparrow, though the Hebrew original does not. This is the progenitor of all the lonely sparrows in Western poetry, including those of Petrarch and Leopardi. See Giovanni Pozzi, *Alternatim* (Milan: Adelphi, 1996), 45–71 and 169–72.

7. In his *Hamlet in Purgatory*, Stephen Greenblatt examines the problem of religious imagination in *Hamlet*, placing it in the historical and cultural context of the period. I wonder whether the author (and the many reviewers) have not overlooked the most important question pertinent to the overall perspective offered by Greenblatt's book as a whole, a question inevitably generated by the book's very argument. Where (if indeed Shakespeare was imagining a place) does Hamlet's soul go after death? In Heaven, one would irresistibly be tempted to respond, alongside the "Good night, sweet prince, / And flights of angels sing thee to thy rest" pronounced by Horatio upon his friend's death (Harold Jenkins' commentary seems to concur). This might well be Horatio's pious *desire,* and as such ought not to be questioned. But Hamlet, from a Christian perspective, is certainly guilty of the elimination of Rosencrantz and Guildenstern (for which, as we have seen, he says that "even in that was heaven ordinant"), and of attempting and finally succeeding in killing Claudius. Though Hamlet and Laertes exchange a strange and partial kind of pardon, Hamlet never explicitly repents for these other sins (which Horatio knows about), nor talks about forgiving his uncle. Neither, then, could Purgatory be his final destination. So does not the scholar Horatio know even the most basic theology, be it Catholic or Protestant? Or does he simply wish to bless Hamlet, as Christians would traditionally do with their dying relatives and friends? And what could Hamlet "say," a few seconds before dying, to "You . . . / That are but mutes or audience to this act," had he the time that "this fell sergeant, Death . . . strict in his arrest" does not leave him?

A single silent tear is enough to save Dante's Buonconte da Montefeltro in *Purgatorio* 5, and, led by God's *angel,* he ends up in Purgatory (while his father Guido, precisely because he has not repented, and notwithstanding a preventive papal absolution, ends up in Hell in *Inferno* 27). Is Hamlet's silence here a sort of confession? Will he, like his father, end up in Purgatory? These are, as far as the text itself is concerned, redundant questions, but fundamental and inevitable for the reader. If we were to read or watch the play not as twenty-first-century critics but as seventeenth-century humans—or, more generally, as Christians—these are precisely the questions that we would pose at the end of the play, having heard Hamlet's father's ghost say at the beginning that he came from Purgatory.

Clearly, Shakespeare is not Dante, and in *Hamlet* (5.2) we find a strange mix of ethical and metaphysical perspectives. When Hamlet kills Claudius, Laertes declares the latter to be "justly served" (an eye for an eye), but he then asks Hamlet for mutual pardon (a Christian gesture). Hamlet replies as a Christian, "Heaven make thee free of it!" After having turned to Horatio with "Had I but time . . . / O, I could tell you," Hamlet begs him to live and "report me and my cause aright / To the unsatisfied," that is, to inform others and to justify his actions. And he insists on this point, speaking of the "wounded name" he will leave behind and imploring his friends to tell his story. Hamlet, in other words, seems concerned with his reputation (and with the political future of Denmark) more than with his own eternal death (or life). His final word is neither Paradise, nor Hell, nor Purgatory but—significantly—"silence."

Chapter 2. *God's Spies*

1. For this tradition, see G. Ravasi, *Giobbe,* 3rd ed. (Rome: Borla, 2005), 108–270.

2. See also Fisch, *The Biblical Presence,* 123–32, and the references therein; and Harold Fisch, *New Stories for Old: Biblical Patterns in the Novel* (London: Palgrave Macmillan, 1998), 100–115.

3. *Hysterica passio* is Lear's own diagnosis, in 2.4.57.

4. See P. Boitani, *Esodi e Odissee* (Naples: Liguori, 2004), 165–66.

5. The parallel path is splendidly described by Fisch in *The Biblical Presence,* 132–42.

6. Compare Dante, *Purgatorio* 30.73: "Ben son, ben son Beatrice."

7. The distinction between "God" and "Gods" is here linguistic and print dependent: it is neither substantial nor cultural. On Christ as sacrifice to God, cf. Ephesians 5:2.

Chapter 3. *Music of the Spheres*

1. T. S. Eliot, "Shakespeares Verskunst," *Der Monat* 2, no. 20 (1950), adapted from a lecture in English partly reproduced in G. Wilson Knight, *Neglected Powers* (New York: Barnes & Noble, 1971), 489–90.

2. See also Isaiah 53:3 (the suffering servant).

3. See 2.1.4 above, and 3.3.9–10: "We cannot but obey / The powers above us."

4. Pericles feeds Tarsus as he declares to Cleon, to "give them life whom hunger starved half dead."

5. With her virtuous words, Marina is able to "alter" even Lysimachus and spur his generosity.

6. T. S. Eliot, *Edinburgh Lectures* II, p. 18 (*The Development of Shakespeare's Verse,* John Davy Hayward Collection of King's College, Cambridge), as quoted

in J. Freeh, "*Pericles* and 'Marina': T. S. Eliot's Search for the Transcendent in Late Shakespeare," in *Shakespeare's Last Plays: Essays in Literature and Politics,* ed. S. W. Smith and T. Curtright (Lanham, MD: Lexington Books, 2002), 112–13.

7. Aristotle, *Poetics* 4.1448b4–6; Sigmund Freud, *Jokes and Their Relation to the Unconscious,* ed. A. Richards (Harmondsworth: Penguin, 1976), 169–71.

8. Euripides, *Helen,* 560.

9. Cf. Dante, *Paradiso* 33.1, where the Virgin Mary is addressed as "figlia di tuo figlio."

10. A. Serpieri, *Pericle, principe di Tiro* (Milan: Garzanti, 2008), 216.

11. Serpieri, *Pericle, principe di Tiro,* 217.

Chapter 4. Divineness

1. The historical source for the plot is Holinshed's *Chronicles.*

2. The plot derives from the ninth *novella* of the second day of Boccaccio's *Decameron,* which Shakespeare perhaps knew through *Frederyke of Jennen* (an English translation of a German tale), and which in any case he modifies in the ending, substituting forgiveness for punishment of the trickster.

3. According to Aristotle, this is the task of tragedy. Compare V. Goldschmidt, *Temps physique et temps tragique chez Aristote* (Paris: Vrin, 1982), 264–65.

Chapter 5. Resurrection

1. For other references in this paragraph, see 3.3.1–2, 56–57; 1.2.418–19; 4.4.25–35, 133–34; 2.3.76; 3.2.118; 4.3.24–26, 41–43. The principal sources for *The Winter's Tale* are Robert Greene's romance *Pandosto,* Sir Philip Sidney's *Arcadia,* and passages from Edmund Spenser's *Faerie Queene.* The epitaph on Giulio Romano's tomb, as cited by Vasari, also proclaims him to be a sculptor. See Giorgio Vasari, *Vite,* ed. L. Bellosi and A. Rossi (Turin: Einaudi, 1981), 837.

2. As Lear had put it, "Thou'dst shun a bear; / But if thy flight lay toward the raging sea, / Thou'dst meet the bear i' the mouth" (3.5.9–11).

3. As the old shepherd tells his son, "thou met'st with things dying, I with things new-born."

4. The full passage runs thus: "What you do, / Still betters what is done. When you speak, sweet, / I'd have you do it ever: when you sing, / I'd have you buy and sell so, so give alms, / Pray so, and, for the ord'ring your affairs, / To sing them too: when you do dance, I wish you / A wave o' th' sea, that you might

ever do / Nothing but that; move still, still so, / And own no other function. Each your doing, / So singular in each particular, / Crowns what you are doing, in the present deeds, / That all your acts are queens."

5. The story of Lazarus anticipates and prefigures, in John, the story of the resurrection of Christ.

6. Is it a coincidence that "Paulina" is a feminine version of "Paul"?

7. The first option is also favored in theatrical productions, in which Hermione's statue can only be a living actress, who needs to be able to play another *fiction*, that of the statue. The reader of the text can give in to the illusion, which could also perfectly be recreated by the tricks of cinema's special effects.

Chapter 6. Epiphany

1. These lines, like the following ones, will be cited by T. S. Eliot in *The Waste Land*.

2. The final part of the prophecy (Isa. 29:9–10) also seems to be consonant with *The Tempest*: "*Stupefy* yourselves and be in a stupor, blind yourselves and be blind! *Be drunk,* but not from wine; stagger, but not from strong drink! For the Lord has poured out upon you a spirit of *deep sleep;* he has closed your eyes, you prophets, and covered your heads, you seers" (emphasis mine). The Geneva Bible, in the margin note for Isaiah 29:1, specifies that the Hebrew word "Ariel" means the lion of God, and the altar, for the altar seems to devour the sacrifice offered to God.

3. The episode is suggested by *Aeneid* 3.209–77, where Aeneas and his men, alighted on the Strophades, prepare a banquet; but as they are about to eat, they are assailed by the harpies, who inhabit those islands and who devour their food. *Everyman* is a morality play printed in England in the fifteenth century: on God's behalf, Death calls Everyman to final judgment.

4. The phrase is the same for the descendants of the couple—"long continuance, and *increasing*" in Juno's words—and for the earth—"earth's *increase*" in Ceres' (4.1.107, 110). Compare Gen. 1:28: "*increase* and multiply" is the version of the Douai-Rheims Bible, that is, the English Catholic Bible, whereas the Geneva Bible has "bring forth frute and multiplie," and the King James has "be fruitful, and multiply."

5. I read the line following the Orgel Shakespeare. But there is still debate as to whether one should read "wife" or "wise." Some copies of the folio have one version, others, the other version.

6. Of course, the "great globe" of line 153 is also a shadow of the Globe Theatre in Elizabethan London.

7. This is an incisive formula that picks up on a topos of Renaissance debate: "on whose *nature / Nurture* can never stick" (emphasis mine).

8. See Jer. 31:35; Amos 8:9; Ezek. 37:12.

9. The opening of tombs and the resurrection of the dead are much stronger in Shakespeare's formulation. He also further highlights them by placing them at the end and climax of Prospero's actions.

10. Virgil here compares the souls of Elysium to bees.

11. The word "indulgence" could suggest a Catholic context.

12. See Plato, *Theaetetus* 155d; Aristotle, *Metaphyics* A2, 982b11–19.

13. Such, as recalled in this passage, is the double Hebrew etymology of "Ariel" according to the Geneva Bible.

14. See Genesis 1:2; *The Tempest* 1.1; Revelation 21:1 and Isaiah 65:17; *The Tempest* 5.1.183.

Conclusion

1. In this context we can bring to mind another crucial episode regarding feet: the washing by Jesus of the disciples' feet before the Last Supper (John 31:3–11). According to Origen (who cites Isaiah and Paul) and the following tradition, this event is a source of *beauty* for those disciples who will announce the Good News. See Origen's commentary on John, 32.77–83 (in *Commentaire sur S. Jean*, vol. 5, ed. C. Blanc [Paris: Cerf, 1992], 220–23).

2. Harold Fisch, *Poetry with a Purpose* (Bloomington: Indiana University Press, 1990), 16–17.

3. On the question of time, space, and motion, see A. Fletcher, *Time, Space and Motion in the Age of Shakespeare* (Cambridge, MA: Harvard University Press, 2007).

4. See also *The Merchant of Venice* 5.1.60–65.

5. The prototypes for this trumpet (in the figural sense given to it in the exegetical tradition) are the trumpets at Joshua's destruction of the walls of Jericho (Josh. 6:20).

6. There is also the unique biblical figure of David, singer of the Psalms, who dances naked before the Ark of the Covenant and is the prototype of the poet dominated by divine ecstasy. Bishop Robert Lowth, who at the end of the eighteenth century was the first to dedicate a book to the study of the Bible as literature (the splendid *De sacra poesi Hebraeorum* [2d ed., Oxford: E Typographeo Clarendoniano, 1821]), applied the Greek terminology of Plato, Aristotle, and Pseudo-Longinus to Hebrew poetry, speaking of the *enthusiasmos* and the *furor* of inspiration necessary to attain the sublime of the Psalms, of the Song of Moses (Deuteronomy 32), and of the books of Job, Isaiah, and Jeremiah.

7. To cite only a few examples of wonder in the Gospels, see Luke 2:18; Mark 6:51; Matthew 8:27, 21:20; Luke 24:12, 24, 37. Note its absence in John.

Selected Bibliography

1. Editions of the Plays with Commentary and Introduction

Included are editions used for quotations in the text, as listed in "Note on the Texts."

Essential Collections:

Teatro completo di William Shakespeare. Ed. G. Melchiori. Milan: Mondadori, 1976–1991.
Romances. Gen. ed. S. Barnet. Introduction by T. Tanner. New York and Toronto: A. Knopf, 1996.
The Oxford Shakespeare. 2nd ed. Ed. S. Wells, G. Taylor, J. Jowett, and W. Montgomery. Oxford: Clarendon Press, 2005.

For the Single Plays:

Hamlet
H. Jenkins, ed. The Arden Shakespeare. 1982.
Il primo Amleto. Ed. A. Serpieri. Venice: Marsilio, 1997.
A. Thompson and N. Taylor, eds. The Arden Shakespeare. 2006.
Amleto. Ed. K. Elam. Milan: Rizzoli, 2007.

King Lear
K. Muir, ed. The Arden Shakespeare. 1952.
R. A. Foakes, ed. The Arden Shakespeare. 1997.

Pericles
F. D. Hoeniger, ed. The Arden Shakespeare. 1963.
P. Edwards, ed. Harmondsworth: Penguin, 1976.
S. Orgel, ed. New York: Penguin, 2001.
R. Warren, ed. Oxford: Clarendon Press, 2003.
S. Gossett, ed. The Arden Shakespeare. 2004.

Cymbeline
J. M. Nosworthy, ed. The Arden Shakespeare. 1955.
R. Hosley, ed. New York: Signet, 1968.
R. Warren, ed. Oxford: Clarendon Press, 1998.
A. R. Braunmuller, ed. Pelican Shakespeare, 2000.

The Winter's Tale
J. H. P. Pafford, ed. The Arden Shakespeare. 1963.
A. Quiller-Couch and J. Dover Wilson, eds. Cambridge: Cambridge University Press, 1968.
Le Conte d'hiver. Trad. Yves Bonnefoi. Paris: Gallimard, 1996.
F. Kermode, ed. 2nd ed. New York: Signet, 1998.
B. A. Mowat and P. Werstine, eds. The New Folger Library Shakespeare, 1998.
S. Orgel, ed. Oxford: Oxford University Press, 1998.

The Tempest
F. Kermode, ed. The Arden Shakespeare. 1954.
A. Barton, ed. Harmondsworth: Penguin, 1968.
S. Orgel, ed. Oxford: Clarendon Press, 1987.
La Tempête. Trans. Y. Bonnefoi. Paris: Gallimard, 1997.
P. Holland, ed. Pelican Shakespeare, 1999.
V. M. Vaughan and A. T. Vaughan, eds. The Arden Shakespeare, 1999.
D. Lindley, ed. Cambridge: Cambridge University Press, 2002.
A. Horowitz. *Prospero's "True Preservers": Peter Brook, Yukio Ninagawa, and Giorgio Strehler—Twentieth-Century Directors Approach Shakespeare's "The Tempest."* Newark: University of Delaware Press, 2004.
La Tempesta. Tradotta e messa in scena da Agostino Lombardo e Giorgio Strehler, ed. R. M. Colombo. Rome: Donzelli, 2007.

2. Books and Critical Essays

The Casebooks (Macmillan) devoted to the romance plays (*Shakespeare's Romances,* ed. A. Thorne) and to the single plays (*Hamlet,* ed. J. Jump; *King Lear,* ed. F. Kermode; *King Lear,* ed. K. Ryan; *The Winter's Tale,* ed. K. Muir; *The Tempest,* ed. D. J. Palmer) contain classic, and still relevant, critical material.

Other important works are, in chronological order:

C. Wordsworth. *Shakespeare and the Bible.* 3rd ed. London: Smith, Elder, & Co., 1880.

E. M. W. Tillyard. *Shakespeare's Last Plays*. London: Chatto and Windus, 1938.

G. Wilson Knight. *The Crown of Life. Essays in Interpretation of Shakespeare's Last Plays*. London: Oxford University Press, 1947.

D. Traversi. *Shakespeare: The Last Phase*. London: Hollis & Carter, 1954.

G. Bullough, ed. *Narrative and Dramatic Sources of Shakespeare*. London: Routledge; New York: Columbia University Press, 1957–1975.

F. Kermode. *William Shakespeare: The Final Plays*. London: Longmans (for the British Council), 1963.

N. Frye. *A Natural Perspective. The Development of Shakespearean Comedy and Romance*. New York: Columbia University Press, 1965.

W. R. Elton. *King Lear and the Gods*. San Marino, CA: The Huntington Library, 1966.

G. Lamming. *Water with Berries*. New York: Holt, Rinehart and Winston, 1971.

H. Felperin. *Shakespearean Romance*. Princeton: Princeton University Press, 1972.

H. Smith. *Shakespeare's Romances: A Study of Some Ways of the Imagination*. San Marino, CA: Huntington Library, 1972.

D. L. Peterson. *Time, Tide, and Tempest: A Study of Shakespeare's Romances*. San Marino, CA: Huntington Library, 1973.

S. Orgel. *The Illusion of Power*. Berkeley: University of California Press, 1975.

F. A. Yates. *Shakespeare's Last Plays*. London: Routledge, 1975.

N. Frye. *The Secular Scripture: A Study of the Structure of Romance*. Cambridge, MA, and London: Harvard University Press, 1976.

B. Mowat. *The Dramaturgy of Shakespeare's Romances*. Athens, GA: University of Georgia Press, 1976.

C. McGinnis Kay and H. E. Jacobs, eds. *Shakespeare's Romances Reconsidered*. Lincoln: University of Nebraska Press, 1978.

N. Fusini. *Il racconto d'inverno*. In *Shakespeare e Johnson, il teatro elisabettiano oggi*, ed. A. Lombardo. Rome: Officina, 1979.

I.-S. Ewbank. "'My Name Is Marina': The Language of Recognition." In P. Edwards, I.-S. Ewbank, and G. K. Hunter, eds., *Shakespeare's Styles: Essays in Honour of Kenneth Muir*. Cambridge: Cambridge University Press, 1980.

C. Frey. *Shakespeare's Vast Romance: A Study of "The Winter's Tale."* Columbia: University of Missouri Press, 1980.

N. Fusini. *La Passione dell'Origine: saggi sul tragico shakesperiano*. Bari: Dedalo Libri, 1981.

A. D. Nuttall. *A New Mimesis: Shakespeare and the Representation of Reality*. London: Methuen, 1983.

F. Marenco. *From Romance to Ritual: Memory and the Community in Shakespeare's Last Plays*. In *Shakespeare Today*, ed. K. Elam. Florence: La Casa Usher, 1984.

J. Dollimore and A. Sinfield, eds. *Political Shakespeare: New Essays in Cultural Materialism.* Manchester: Manchester University Press, 1985.

R. S. White. *"Let Wonder Seem Familiar": Endings in Shakespeare's Romance Vision.* London: Athlone Press, 1985.

L. Barkan. *The Gods Made Flesh: Metamorphosis and the Pursuit of Paganism.* New Haven and London: Yale University Press, 1986.

N. Frye. *On Shakespeare.* Ed. R. Sandler. New Haven and London: Yale University Press, 1986.

A. Lombardo. *Il testo e la sua performance (Per una critica imperfetta).* Rome: Editori Riuniti, 1986.

R. Ornstein. *Shakespeare's Comedies: From Roman Farce to Romantic Mystery.* Cranbury, NJ: Associated University Presses, 1986.

R. Nevo. *Shakespeare's Other Language.* New York: Methuen, 1987.

L. Marcus. *Puzzling Shakespeare: Local Reading and Its Discontents.* Berkeley: University of California Press, 1988.

R. M. Adams. *Shakespeare: The Four Romances.* New York: Norton, 1989.

M. Hunt. *Shakespeare's Romance of the Word.* Lewisburg, PA: Bucknell University Press, 1990.

S. Greenblatt. *Marvelous Possessions: the Wonder of the New World.* Chicago: University of Chicago Press, 1991.

C. Marshall. *Shakespearean Eschatology: Last Things and Last Plays.* Carbondale and Edwardsville: Southern Illinois University Press, 1991.

H. W. Fawkner. *Shakespeare's Miracle Plays: "Pericles", "Cymbeline" and "The Winter's Tale."* London: Associated University Presses, 1992.

S. Greenblatt. *Learning to Curse.* New York and London: Routledge, 1992.

M. Mincoff. *Things Supernatural and Causeless: Shakespearean Romance.* Newark: University of Delaware Press, 1992.

P. M. Simonds. *Myth, Emblem, and Music in Shakespeare's "Cymbeline": An Iconographic Reconstruction.* London: Associated University Presses, 1992.

B. Sokolova. *Shakespeare's Romances as Interrogative Texts: Their Alienation Strategies and Ideology.* Lewiston, NY: Edwin Mellen, 1992.

L. Barkan. "The Beholder's Tale: Ancient Sculpture, Renaissance Narratives." *Representations* 44 (1993): 133–66.

C. Peltrault, ed. *Shakespeare: "La Tempête": Études Critiques.* Besançon: Université de Franche-Comté, 1993.

A. Barton. *Essays, Mainly Shakespearean.* Cambridge: Cambridge University Press, 1994.

J. Gillies. *Shakespeare and the Geography of Difference,* Cambridge: Cambridge University Press, 1994.

G. Melchiori. *Shakespeare.* Bari: Laterza, 1994.

L. Barkan. "Making Pictures Speak: Renaissance Art, Elizabethan Literature, Modern Scholarship." *Renaissance Quarterly* 48 (1995): 326–51.

T. G. Bishop. *Shakespeare and the Theatre of Wonder*. Cambridge: Cambridge University Press, 1996.

R. Henke. *Pastoral Transformations: Italian Tragicomedy and Shakespeare's Late Plays*. London: Associated University Presses, 1997.

S. Palfrey. *Late Shakespeare. A New World of Words*. Oxford: Clarendon Press, 1997.

Y. Bonnefoy. *Shakespeare et Yeats*. Paris: Mercure de France, 1998.

J. Richards and J. Knowles, eds. *Shakespeare's Late Plays: New Readings*. Edinburgh: Edinburgh University Press, 1999.

T. Rist. *Shakespeare's Romances and the Politics of Counter-Reformation*. Lewiston, NY: Edwin Mellen, 1999.

K. Ryan, ed. *Shakespeare: The Last Plays*. London and New York: Longman, 1999.

R. S. White, ed. *"The Tempest": Contemporary Critical Essays*. Basingstoke: Macmillan, 1999.

B. A. Adams, *Coming-to-Know: Recognition and the Complex Plot in Shakespeare*. New York and Berlin: Peter Lang, 2000.

H. Bloom, ed. *Shakespeare's Romances*. Philadelphia: Chelsea House, 2000.

G. Graff and J. Phelan, eds. *The Tempest*. Boston: Bedford/St Martin's Press, 2000.

P. Hulme and W. Sherman, eds. *The Tempest and Its Travels*. London: Reaktion, 2000.

F. Kermode. *Shakespeare's Language*. Harmondsworth: Penguin, 2000.

S. Marx. *Shakespeare and the Bible*. Oxford: Oxford University Press, 2000.

V. B. Richmond. *Shakespeare, Catholicism, and Romance*. London and New York: Continuum, 2000.

D. Skeele, ed. *"Pericles": Critical Essays*. New York and London: Garland, 2000.

S. Greenblatt. *Hamlet in Purgatory*. Princeton: Princeton University Press, 2001.

M. D. Friedman. *"The World Must Be Peopled": Shakespeare's Comedies of Forgiveness*. London: Associated University Presses, 2002.

A. Lombardo. *La grande conchiglia. Due studi su "La Tempesta."* Rome: Bulzoni, 2002.

S. W. Smith and T. Curtright, eds. *Shakespeare's Last Plays: Essays in Literature and Politics*. Lanham, MD: Lexington Books (Rowman & Littlefield), 2002.

W. H. Auden. *The Sea and the Mirror*. Ed. A. Kirsch. Princeton: Princeton University Press, 2003.

C. A. Bernthal. *The Trial of Man: Christianity and Judgment in the World of Shakespeare*. Wilmington, DE: ISI Books, 2003.

S. Cavell. *Disowning Knowledge in Seven Plays of Shakespeare*. Cambridge and New York: Cambridge University Press, 2003.

M. P. Jackson. *Defining Shakespeare: "Pericles" as Test Case.* Oxford: Oxford University Press, 2003.

M. Jones-Davies. "*Cymbeline* and the Sleep of Faith." In A. Findlay and R. Wilson, eds., *Theatre and Religion: Lancastrian Shakespeare*, 197–217. Manchester: Manchester University Press, 2003.

D. N. Beauregard and D. Taylor, eds. *Shakespeare and the Culture of Christianity in Early Modern England.* New York: Fordham University Press, 2004.

H. Cooper. *The English Romance in Time: Transforming Motifs from Geoffrey of Monmouth to the Death of Shakespeare.* Oxford: Oxford University Press, 2004.

N. Fusini. *Donne fatali. Ofelia, Desdemona, Cleopatra.* Rome: Bulzoni, 2005.

B. Batson. *Shakespeare's Christianity: The Protestant and Catholic Poetics of "Julius Caesar", "Macbeth" and "Hamlet."* Waco, TX: Baylor University Press, 2006.

B. Groves. *Texts and Traditions: Religion in Shakespeare, 1592–1604.* Oxford: Clarendon Press, 2006.

C. McGinn. *Shakespeare's Philosophy: Discovering the Meaning Behind the Plays.* New York: Harper Collins, 2006.

R. McDonald. *Shakespeare's Late Style.* Cambridge: Cambridge University Press, 2006.

A. Tigner. "*The Winter's Tale:* Gardens and the Marvels of Transformation." *English Literary Renaissance* 36 (2006): 114–34.

C. J. Cobb. *The Staging of Romance in Later Shakespeare: Text and Theatrical Technique.* Newark: University of Delaware Press, 2007.

J. D. Cox. *Seeming Knowledge: Shakespeare and Skeptical Faith.* Waco, TX: Baylor University Press, 2007.

A. Fletcher. *Time, Space, and Motion in the Age of Shakespeare.* Cambridge, MA, and London: Harvard University Press, 2007.

R. Lyne. *Shakespeare's Late Work.* Oxford: Oxford University Press, 2007.

G. McMullan. *Shakespeare and the Idea of Late Writing: Authorship in the Proximity of Death.* Cambridge: Cambridge University Press, 2007.

A. D. Nuttall. *Shakespeare the Thinker.* New Haven and London: Yale University Press, 2007.

D. N. Beauregard. *Catholic Theology in Shakespeare's Plays.* Newark: University of Delaware Press, 2008.

G. Sacerdoti. *Nuovo cielo, nuova terra.* Reprint. Rome: Edizioni di Storia e Letteratura, 2008.

C. M. S. Alexander, ed. *The Cambridge Companion to Shakespeare's Last Plays.* Cambridge: Cambridge University Press, 2009.

A. Gurr. *The Shakespearean Stage, 1574–1642.* 4th ed. Cambridge: Cambridge University Press, 2009.

N. Fusini. *Di vita si muore: Lo spettacolo delle passioni nel teatro di Shakespeare.* Milan: Mondadori, 2010.

T. Tanner. *Prefaces to Shakespeare*. Cambridge, MA: Belknap Press of Harvard University Press, 2010.

S. Beckwith. *Shakespeare and the Grammar of Forgiveness*. Ithaca, NY, and London: Cornell University Press, 2011.

K. Jackson and A. F. Marotti, eds. *Shakespeare and Religion: Early Modern and Postmodern Perspectives*. Notre Dame: University of Notre Dame Press, 2011.

3. On Music

J. H. Long. *Shakespeare's Use of Music*. Gainesville: University of Florida Press, 1955.

W. H. Auden. "Music in Shakespeare." In *The Dyer's Hand and Other Essays*, 500–527. London: Faber, 1957.

J. Hollander. *The Untuning of the Sky: Ideas of Music in English Poetry, 1500–1700*. Princeton: Princeton University Press, 1961.

E. J. Dent. "Shakespeare and Music." In *Companion to Shakespeare Studies*, ed. H. Granville-Barker and G. B. Harrison, 137–61. Cambridge: Cambridge University Press, 1962.

C. M. Dunn. "The Function of Music in Shakespeare's Romances." *Shakespeare Quarterly* 20 (1969): 391–405.

F. W. Sternfeld. "Shakespeare and Music." In *A New Companion to Shakespeare Studies*, ed. K. Muir and S. Schoenbaum, 157–67. Cambridge: Cambridge University Press, 1971.

D. Lindley. *Shakespeare and Music*. London: Thomson Learning, 2005.

C. R. Wilson and M. Calore. *Music in Shakespeare: A Dictionary*. New York and London: Continuum, 2005.

Index

Acts 27:34, 91
Adam and Eve, 6, 94–95, 112, 114, 122
Aeneid (Virgil), 13, 101
  3.209–77, 137n.3
  4.700–701, 103
  6.707–9, 111
Alexander the Great, 18, 19
amen
  Doctor Faustus (Marlowe), 22
  Hamlet, 3, 21
  Paradiso (Dante), 86
  The Tempest, 3, 114, 123
Amos 8:9, 138n.8
Antony and Cleopatra (Shakespeare), 65
apocalypse, 105–6
Apollonius of Tyre, 42, 43
Aristotle, 50, 87, 118, 130
  Metaphysics A2, 982b11–19, 138n.12
  Poetics 4.1448b4–6, 50, 82, 136n.7
artistic mimesis, 87, 119
art. *See also* music
  The Tempest, 119–20
  The Winter's Tale, 78–83, 85, 87, 119
As You Like It (Shakespeare) 2.7.140–67, 106

Bacchae (Euripides), 25
baptism, 93

beauty
  concluding remarks, 126–28
  Cymbeline, 94
  Hamlet, 12–13
  Pericles, 94
  Romans 10:15, 127
  salvation and, 127
  The Tempest, 94–95, 118–19, 126–27
  in Jesus' washing the disciples' feet, 138n.1
  The Winter's Tale, 94

Calvin, John, 2
Coleridge, Samuel, 125
Commedia (Dante). See *Divine Comedy*
communion
  King Lear, 36
  The Tempest, 102
compassion
  King Lear, 5, 7
  The Tempest, 108
  The Winter's Tale, 83
Confessio Amantis (Gower), 42
consummation
  Cymbeline, 5, 62–64, 129
  Hamlet, 4–5, 16–18, 64, 88, 99
  King Lear, 5, 38–39
  The Tempest, 99, 106
  The Winter's Tale, 88

Convivio (Dante) 4.25.5, 130
1 Corinthians, 30
  3:18–19, 30
  15:12–13, 125
  15:36, 81
  15:52, 129
Cymbeline (Shakespeare)
  2.3.19–25, 129
  2.4, 65
  2.4.108–10, 65
  2.4.133–41, 66
  3.3, 60
  3.3.27–44, 60
  3.6, 60
  3.7, 60
  4.2, 60
  4.2.51–58, 61
  4.2.203–8, 62
  4.2.209–11, 62
  4.2.218–29, 62
  4.2.258–81, 62–63
  4.2.299–302, 64
  4.4, 60
  5.2, 66
  5.2.369–70, 70
  5.4.3–29, 66–67
  5.4.99–103, 72
  5.4.144–51, 67
  5.4.183–88, 68
  5.5, 68
  5.5.382–98, 70
  5.5.437–43, 72–73
  5.5.467–68, 72
  5.5.471–77, 58, 73
  the feminine in, 61–62, 73
  grace of Gospels reflected in, 7–8
  music in, 129
  space and time, motion and unity
    in, 128
Dante Alighieri, 50, 53, 54, 86, 107,
  130, 132, 134, 135n.6 (ch. 2),
  136n.9. *See also Convivo; Divine
  Comedy*

David, biblical figure, 138n.6
Des Cannibales (Montaigne), 96
Deuteronomy 32, 138n.6
devil(s)
  Inferno (Dante), 107
  The Tempest, 4, 6, 97, 107, 115, 119,
    121
Dialogues of the Dead (Lucian), 19
Divine Comedy (Dante), 86, 132
  Inferno 21–22, 107
  Inferno 27, 134n.7
  Paradiso (music of), 53
  Paradiso 1.70–71, 54
  Paradiso 14, 86
  Paradiso 14.61–66, 86
  Paradiso 24.64–65, 86
  Paradiso 33.1, 136n.9
  Purgatorio 5, 134n.7
  Purgatorio 30.73, 135n.6 (ch. 2)
divine inspiration, 71, 132, 138n.6
divine justice
  Cymbeline, 71–72
  Hamlet, 3
  Job, 25–26
  King Lear, 30–33
  The Tempest, 101, 120
divineness
  Cymbeline, 4, 61, 71, 73
  Hamlet, 15
  King Lear, 28–29
  Pericles, 55
  The Tempest, 4, 109–12, 122
Doctor Faustus (Marlowe), 21–22, 101
  A.1.12, 16
  A.1.37, 22
Don Giovanni (Mozart), 102

Ecclesiastes, 39
  3:11, 127
ecstasy, 53, 83, 138n.6. *See also* divine
  inspiration
ekplexis, in *The Tempest,* 95. *See also*
  wonder

Eliot, T. S., 42, 48
endurance. *See patientia*
Ephesians 5:2, 135n.3
epiphany, *The Tempest*, 93–95, 98–99, 112–13
eros/carnal knowledge
    Cymbeline, 59–60, 65–66
    The Tempest, 117
Euripides, 54
    Bacchae, 25
    Helen, 8, 51
Everyman, 101
evil
    deliverance from, 116
    Job, 25, 26
    The Tempest, 6, 8, 116, 118, 121, 123
    The Winter's Tale, 77
Ezekiel 37:12, 138n.8

faith, *The Winter's Tale*, 83, 86, 88
fall of the sparrow
    Hamlet, 20–23
    Job, 26
    King Lear, 38
    progenitors of, 134n.6
father-daughter relationships
    King Lear, 6, 26–27, 34–39, 52, 95
    Pericles, 41, 43, 48–53
    The Tempest, 3, 91, 92, 94–95, 117
father-son relationships
    King Lear, 27, 31–32, 38, 112
    The Tempest, 6, 117
Faust (Goethe), 101
the feminine
    concluding remarks, 126
    Cymbeline, 61–62, 73
    grace of, 61, 112
    Pericles, 61
    Shakespeare's use of, 8
    The Winter's Tale, 61
Fisch, Harold, 127–28
Florio, John, 96

forgiveness
    Cymbeline, 5
    Hamlet, 2, 5, 134n.7
    King Lear, 5, 6, 31, 33, 36–37, 112
    reflected in romances, 2
    The Tempest, 108, 110, 112, 115–16, 122–23
    The Winter's Tale, 6, 88
Fortune
    Pericles, 44
    The Tempest, 91, 95, 114, 120
Freud, Sigmund, 50
fulfillment. *See also* consummation
    Cymbeline, 62–64
    Hamlet, 64
    King Lear, 5, 38–39
    reflected in romances, 4–5
    The Winter's Tale, 88

Gabriel, the angel, 86
Genesis, 7, 104, 121–22, 127
    1:2, 138n.14
    1:16, 122
    1:28, 137n.4
    beauty in, 127
God
    man as
    —*King Lear*, 28–29
    —*The Tempest*, 109–12, 122
    questioning of, 25–26, 29, 71–72
    spies of, 5, 37–38, 52, 132
God-human relationships
    Hamlet, 3, 12
    King Lear, 3
    Pericles, 3–4
Goethe (*Faust*), 101
goodness
    Cymbeline, 69
    Hamlet, 2
    music calling for, 119
    Pericles, 47–48
    reflected in romances, 2
    The Tempest, 119

goodness and beauty united
  (*kalokagathia*)
  concluding remarks, 127
  Cymbeline, 94
  Pericles, 94
  The Tempest, 94–95, 118–19
  The Winter's Tale, 94
Gorgias, 16
Gower, John, 42, 44, 47
  Confessio Amantis, 42
grace
  Cymbeline, 7, 61
  the feminine in, 12, 61
  Pericles, 4, 8, 54
  reflected in romances, 5
  The Tempest, 99, 112, 114, 116
  The Winter's Tale, 82, 85
Greenblatt, Stephen (*Hamlet in
  Purgatory*), 134n.7

Habakkuk 2:1, 38
Hamlet (Shakespeare)
  1.2.76–86, 11–12
  1.2.129–37, 12
  1.5.9–13, 133n.1
  2.2.294–308, 12–13
  2.2.544–56, 13–14
  3.1.56–68, 16–17
  3.1.78–85, 17–18
  4.4.32–46, 15–16
  4.6.14–28, 10
  4.7.166–67, 133n.3
  5.1.205–8, 19
  5.1.247–51, 20
  5.1.264–66, 20
  5.2, 107
  5.2.10–11, 21
  5.2.48, 22
  5.2.215–20, 20
  5.2.343, 21
  amen in ending of, 3
  Gospels reflected in, 7–8
  religious imagination in, 134n.7

Handel, George Frideric, 129
happiness
  concluding remarks, 126
  Cymbeline, 126
  ephemeral nature of, 126
  Hamlet, 2
  Pericles, 55
  reflected in romances, 1–2, 8
  The Tempest, 95, 98–99, 112,
    114
  The Winter's Tale, 78–79, 86, 95
Hebrews 11:1, 86
Helen (Euripides), 8, 51
Henry VIII (Shakespeare), 133n.1
Homer, 7
  The Odyssey, 61, 132
hope
  Cymbeline, 73
  The Tempest, 101, 113
  The Winter's Tale, 85

Inferno (Dante)
  21–22, 107
  27, 134n.7
Isaiah
  29:1, 137n.2
  29:6, 100
  29:8, 100
  29:9–10, 137n.2
  52:7, 127, 128
  53:3, 135n.2
  65:17, 138n.14
  65:17–18, 113
  beauty in, 127, 128, 131

Jacobus de Voragine (*Legenda aurea*),
    42–43
James I, 2, 58
Jeremiah 31:35, 138n.8
Jerome, Saint (Vulgate), 21
Jesus, 49
  beauty in words and actions of, 126,
    138n.1

call to readiness, 21, 38
Cordelia compared, 34, 36, 37
Hamlet's words of, 21
Job juxtaposed, 27
Lear compared, 25, 30, 37
Mariana compared, 48–53
patientia of, 39, 50
Pericles compared, 46, 55
Prospero compared, 111
Job, biblical figure
  Lear compared, 25–30
  patientia of, 28, 39
  Pericles compared, 5, 44, 46
Job, Book of
  5:13, 30
  20:6–8, 106
  38:2–4, 26
  42:3–5, 26
  42:10–17, 26
  Cymbeline's echo of, 64
  Hamlet's echo of, 64
  patientia in, 39
  questioning the divine in, 25–26,
    29, 71–72
  wonder in, 132
John, Gospel of, 50, 55
  11:1–44, 84
  19:30, 17
  31:3–11, 138n.1
  absence of wonder in, 138n.7
  grace in, 5
1 John
  1:8, 21
  3:14, 86
Johnson, Robert, 93, 110–11
Jonah, biblical figure, 41, 43
Joseph, biblical figure, 121
Joshua 6:20, 138n.5
Judas, biblical figure, 75, 101
justice, divine
  Cymbeline, 71–72
  Hamlet, 3
  Job, 25–26

King Lear, 30–33
The Tempest, 101, 120

kairós, 80, 83
kalokagathia. See also beauty
  concluding remarks, 127
  Cymbeline, 94
  Pericles, 94
  The Tempest, 94–95, 118–19
  The Winter's Tale, 94
King Lear (Shakespeare)
  2.4.57, 135n.3
  2.4.106, 28
  2.4.159ff., 28
  2.4.162ff., 28
  2.4.228, 28
  2.4.273–75, 27
  2.4.276–78, 27–28
  2.4.280–84, 28
  2.4.284–88, 28
  3.2.1–9, 28–29
  3.2.19–20, 28
  3.2.37, 28
  3.4.6–14, 29
  3.4.28–36, 30
  3.4.103–11, 30–31
  3.4.149–50, 31
  3.4.158ff, 29
  3.4.167–68, 31
  3.4.174, 31
  3.5.9–11, 136n.2
  3.7.90–91, 31
  4.1.21–24, 31
  4.1.36–37, 31
  4.1.64–70, 32
  4.4.23–24, 34
  4.6.72–74, 38
  4.6.75–77, 32
  4.6.180–85, 34
  4.6.206–8, 34
  4.7, 34
  4.7.45–48, 35
  4.7.46, 36

King Lear (Shakespeare) (*cont.*)
  4.7.59–70, 35–36
  5.2.11, 38
  5.3.8–19, 37
  5.3.20–21, 38
  Gospels reflected in, 7–8
  Job as paradigm of, 25–26, 27–30
  Pericles compared, 50, 52
  space and time, motion and unity
    in, 35
knowledge
  of evil, *The Winter's Tale*, 77
  true, *King Lear*, 33, 35–36
knowledge, erotic
  Cymbeline, 59–60, 65–66
  Pericles, 41
  The Tempest, 117

Lazarus, biblical figure, 6, 42, 84–85
Legenda aurea (Jacobus de Voragine),
  42–43
Life of Alexander (Plutarch), 19
Lord's Prayer, 2, 116
love
  contract of, 103–5
  Cymbeline, 72
  of the divine, 72
  happiness and invincibility of, 55,
    78–79, 86, 95, 98–99, 112, 114
  Pericles, 55
  The Tempest, 95, 98–99, 103–5, 112,
    114
  The Winter's Tale, 78–79, 86, 88,
    95
Lucian (*Dialogues of the Dead*), 19
Luke, Gospel of, 2, 5
  2:18, 138n.7
  2:49, 34
  12:6, 21
  12:35–40, 133n.5
  24:12, 138n.7
  24:24, 138n.7
  24:37, 138n.7

Marcus Aurelius, 19
Mark 6:51, 138n.7
Marlowe, Christopher (*Doctor
  Faustus*), 16, 21–22, 101
  A.1.12, 16
  A.1.37, 22
Martha, biblical figure, 42, 84
Mary, mother of Jesus, 8, 86
Mary Magdalene, biblical figure, 42,
  43, 49, 50, 55
Mary Magdalen (play), 43
Matthew, Gospel of, 2
  3:17, 52
  5:3–12, 44
  6:14–15, 116
  8:27, 138n.7
  10:29, 20
  18:22, 112
  21:20, 138n.7
  24:44, 133n.5
The Merchant of Venice (Shakespeare),
  138n.4
  5.1.58–65, 53–54
mercy
  Cymbeline, 66–67
  Hamlet, 22–23
  King Lear, 33
  The Tempest, 116, 122
Metamorphoses (Ovid)
  7.198–209, 108
  7.206, 110
  7.208–9, 109–10
Metaphysics (Aristotle) A2,
  982b11–19, 138n.12
A Midsummer Night's Dream
  (Shakespeare), 131–32
  5.1.9–20, 131
Montaigne, Michel de, 79,
  121
  Des Cannibales, 96
Moses, biblical figure, 132
Mozart, Wolfgang Amadeus (*Don
  Giovanni*), 102

music
  concluding remarks, 129–30
  Cymbeline, 129
  A Midsummer Night's Dream, 53–54
  motion of, 129
  Paradiso (Dante), 53, 54
  Pericles, 53–55, 110, 129
  The Tempest, 92–93, 94, 100, 101,
    102, 105, 108–11, 129–30
  The Winter's Tale, 53, 83–84, 87, 129

nature
  The Tempest, 102–3, 106, 109, 117
  The Winter's Tale, 78–83, 87, 119
Nicene Creed, 86

The Odyssey (Homer), 61, 132
Origen, 138n.1
Ovid, 121
  Metamorphoses 7.198–209, 108
  Metamorphoses 7.206, 110
  Metamorphoses 7.208–9, 109–10

Palazzo Te, 7, 82
paradise
  Hamlet, 15
  King Lear, 36, 37
  The Tempest, 2, 7, 95, 102–6,
    116–17, 122
Paradiso (Dante)
  1.70–71, 54
  14, 86
  14.61–66, 86
  24.64–65, 86
  33.1, 136n.7
  music in, 53, 54
Parmenides, 16
patientia
  Cymbeline, 4–5, 72
  Hamlet, 4–5
  of Job, 28
  King Lear, 4–5, 28–32, 34, 38–39
  Pericles, 4, 44, 46, 49–50

The Tempest, 4, 122
The Winter's Tale, 4, 83
Paul, the apostle, 5, 7, 85, 128
peace, *pulchritudo* and, 127
Pentateuch, 132
Pericles (Shakespeare)
  1.4.85–96, 45
  2 Chorus, line 3, 45
  2 Chorus, line 9, 45
  2 Chorus, line 12, 45
  2.1.1–11, 44–45
  2.1.37, 44
  2.1.59–62, 45
  2.1.71–77, 45
  2.1.122, 44
  2.3.43–44, 45
  2.3.44–45, 47
  2.5.26, 53
  2.5.28, 53
  3.1.1–6, 45–46
  3.1.10–14, 46
  3.1.22–26, 46
  3.1.46, 44
  3.2.86–89, 53
  4.1.13–20, 47
  4.4.29–31, 44
  4.4.47–48, 44
  4.6.108, 47
  4.6.112, 47
  5 Chorus, lines 3–7, 47
  5.1.103–5, 48
  5.1.119–25, 49
  5.1.134–41, 50
  5.1.142–44, 50
  5.1.152–55, 51
  5.1.161–63, 51
  5.1.190–99, 51–52
  5.1.205–7, 52
  5.1.212–15, 52
  5.1.231–33, 53
  5.2.13–14, 55
  5.2.31–34, 55
  5.3.40–44, 55

Pericles (Shakespeare) (*cont.*)
  Apollonius's story in, 42, 43
  the feminine in, 61
  Gospels reflected in, 7–8
  Job, theme in, 46
  Lear compared, 50, 52
  Mary Magdalene, legend in, 42,
    43, 49
  mentioned, 90
  music in, 53–55, 110, 129
  space and time, motion and unity
    in, 128
Peter, the apostle, 42–43
2 Peter 3:13, 113
Philippians 2:7, 122
Philoctetes (Sophocles), 25
Plato, 18, 118, 127, 130
  Theatetus 155d, 138n.12
Plutarch (*Life of Alexander*), 19
Poetics (Aristotle)
  4.1448b4–6, 50, 82, 136n.7
providence
  Doctor Faustus (Marlowe), 22
  Hamlet, 2, 20–23, 114
  King Lear, 38
  reflected in romances, 2
  The Tempest, 2, 90, 95, 114, 120, 123
Psalms
  102:3–4, 22
  102:7, 22
  102:12–13, 22–23
  107:25, 91
  111:3, 127
  wonder in, 132
pulchritudo (beauty). *See also* beauty
  concluding remarks, 126–27
  The Tempest, 119, 126–27
Purgatorio (Dante)
  5, 134n.7
  30.73, 135n.6 (ch. 2)
purgatory
  Hamlet, 2, 18, 133n.1, 134n.7
  Purgatorio 5 (Dante), 134n.7

  The Tempest, 2
  The Winter's Tale, 88
Puttenham, George, 131

Raphael, 7
rebirth. *See also* resurrection
  Cymbeline, 71
  The Tempest, 114
  The Winter's Tale, 78, 80–81
recognition
  Cymbeline, 3, 66, 68–71
  King Lear, 3, 33–36, 39
  Pericles, 3, 48–53
  reflected in romances, 3
  The Tempest, 115–16
  The Winter's Tale, 3, 80
redemption
  Cymbeline, 66–67
  King Lear, 34, 37
  The Tempest, 119
  The Winter's Tale, 84
repentance
  Cymbeline, 5, 66
  Hamlet, 5, 134n.7
  Inferno 27 (Dante), 134n.7
  The Tempest, 101–2, 122–23
  The Winter's Tale, 5–6, 77, 88
resurrection
  concluding remarks, 125
  Cymbeline, 64, 66, 71
  Hamlet, 17–19, 85
  King Lear, 32, 34–39
  Paradiso (Dante), 86
  Pericles, 43, 47, 49–52, 54–55,
    110
  The Tempest, 109–10
  The Winter's Tale, 81, 83–88
Revelation, 122
  21:1, 113, 138n.14
revelation. *See also* epiphany, *The
    Tempest*
  Cymbeline, 68–71
  The Tempest, 3, 90

Romano, Giulio, 7, 76, 82, 84, 119
Romans
  6:23, 21
  10:15, 127
  12:1, 38
Romeo and Juliet (Shakespeare), 64

sacrifice
  Ephesians 5:2, 135n.7
  Isaiah 29:9–10, 137n.2
  King Lear, 5, 7, 38
  Pericles, 54
salvation
  Cymbeline, 73
  Isaiah 52:7, 127
  pulchritudo and, 127
  The Tempest, 119, 121
  The Winter's Tale, 85
self-knowledge
  Hamlet, 15–16, 36
  King Lear, 32–34, 36–37
  transforming the romances, 5
Septuagint (Genesis), 127
Shakespeare, William
  Bible used by, 2
  divine inspiration of, 54
  feminine form used by, 8
  Gospels reflected in romances of,
    5, 6–8
  imagination, ideas dominating,
    3
  religious beliefs, 2
  themes and forms inspiring, 1–5
Sidney, Philip, 131
Socrates, 68
Solomon, biblical figure, 86
Song of Moses (Deut. 32), 138n.6
Song of Songs 4:1, 127
Sophocles (*Philoctetes*), 25
space and time, motion and unity in
  Cymbeline, 128
  King Lear, 35
  Pericles, 128

The Tempest, 89, 128–29
The Winter's Tale, 128
the sparrow. *See* fall of the sparrow
spy of God, 3, 37, 52, 85, 132

The Tempest (Shakespeare)
  1.1, 138n.14
  1.2.136–38, 121
  1.2.159, 114
  1.2.180–85, 120
  1.2.217, 91
  1.2.227–29, 91
  1.2.321–22, 121
  1.2.335–36, 121–22
  1.2.374–80, 92
  1.2.392–97, 92
  1.2.399–405, 93
  1.2.422, 114
  2.1.271–75, 101
  2.2.167–72, 97
  3.1.92–94, 99
  3.2.133–41, 99–100
  3.3.53, 120
  4.1.60–75, 102–3
  4.1.107, 137n.4
  4.1.110, 137n.4
  4.1.110–17, 104
  4.1.122–24, 104
  4.1.146–63, 105–6
  4.1.152–54, 122
  4.1.188–89, 107
  5.1.33–57, 108–9
  5.1.88–94, 110
  5.1.106–9, 111
  5.1.158–62, 111
  5.1.181–84, 113
  5.1.183, 138n.14
  5.1.187, 114
  5.1.189, 114, 120
  5.1.200–204, 114
  amen in ending of, 3
  Epilogue, 13–20, 116
  Gospels reflected in, 7

The Tempest (Shakespeare) (*cont.*)
  Lord's Prayer in, 116
  music in, 92–93, 94, 100, 101, 102,
    105, 108–11, 129–30
  space and time, motion and unity
    in, 89, 128–29
Theatetus (Plato) 155d, 138n.12
Thomas, the apostle, 55, 85
2 Timothy 1:10, 84
transcendence
  Cymbeline, 60, 71–73
  King Lear, 37
  Pericles, 53–54, 128–29
transfiguration
  Cymbeline, 71
  King Lear, 38, 39
  Pericles, 52–53, 55
Twelfth Night (Shakespeare), 3
The Two Noble Kinsmen
    (Shakespeare), 133n.1

the ultra-terrestrial, beyond life,
    48–49, 53, 54

Virgil, 7, 121
  Aeneid, 13, 101
  Aeneid 3.209–77, 137n.3
  Aeneid 4.700–701, 103
  Aeneid 6.707–9, 111
Vulgate of Saint Jerome, 21

the Way, the Truth, and the Life, 6,
    47–49, 52
The Winter's Tale (Shakespeare)
  2.1.22–25, 76
  2.1.38–45, 76–77

3.2.151–55, 77
3.3.108–10, 78
4.4.79–85, 78
4.4.88–97, 78–79
4.4.116–27, 79
4.4.135–46, 80
5.2.9–19, 80
5.2.28, 76
5.2.61–62, 76
5.2.92–100, 81
5.2.94–98, 76
5.3.98–103, 84
5.3.115–17, 85
5.3.117, 76
5.3.139–41, 85
the feminine in, 61
mentioned, 90
music in, 53, 83–84, 87,
    129
space and time, motion and unity
    in, 128
wisdom
  Cymbeline, 67–68
  divine, questioning of, 25–26,
    71–72
  Hamlet, 68
  King Lear, 33, 34–36
wonder
  concluding remarks, 130–32
  Cymbeline, 130
  in the Gospels, 138n.7
  Pericles, 130
  The Tempest, 95, 118, 122, 130
  The Winter's Tale, 130

Zephaniah 1:15–16, 129

Piero Boitani is professor of comparative literature at the University of Rome "La Sapienza." He is the author of numerous books, including *The Genius to Improve an Invention: Literary Transitions* (University of Notre Dame Press, 2002).

www.ingramcontent.com/pod-product-compliance
Ingram Content Group UK Ltd.
Pitfield, Milton Keynes, MK11 3LW, UK
UKHW030708300425
458010UK00001B/28